Normal Sucks

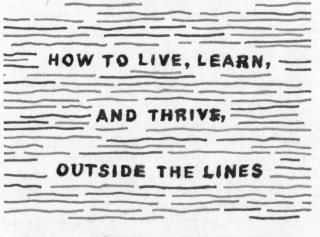

HOW TO LIVE, LEARN,

AND THRIVE,

OUTSIDE THE LINES

Jonathan Mooney

A Holt Paperback
Henry Holt and Company
New York

NORMAL SUCKS. Copyright © 2019 by Jonathan Mooney. All rights reserved. Printed in the United States of America. For information, address Henry Holt and Company, 120 Broadway, New York, NY 10271.

www.henryholt.com

A Holt Paperback® and Ⓗ® are registered trademarks of Macmillan Publishing, LLC.

Designed by Maura Fadden Rosenthal

The Library of Congress has cataloged the hardcover edition as follows:

Names: Mooney, Jonathan, author.
Title: Normal sucks : how to live, learn, and thrive outside the lines / Jonathan
    Mooney.
Description: First edition. | New York : Henry Holt and Company, [2019]
Identifiers: LCCN 2018053025 | ISBN 9781250190161 (hardcover)
Subjects: LCSH: Mooney, Jonathan. | People with disabilities. | Learning
    disabled—United States—Biography.
Classification: LCC HV1568 .M65 2019 | DDC 305.9/084092 [B]—dc23
LC record available at https://lccn.loc.gov/2018053025

ISBN: 978-1-250-77126-1 (trade paperback)
ISBN: 978-1-250-19017-8 (ebook)

Our books may be purchased in bulk for promotional, educational, or business use. Please contact your local bookseller or the Macmillan Corporate and Premium Sales Department at 1-800-221-7945, extension 5442, or by email at MacmillanSpecialMarkets@macmillan.com.

Originally published in hardcover in 2019 by Henry Holt and Company

First Holt Paperbacks Edition 2023

10 9 8 7 6

Normal
Sucks

Also by Jonathan Mooney

The Short Bus: A Journey Beyond Normal

Learning Outside the Lines (with David Cole)

To Becky, still my life, my love, after all these years; nothing is possible without you and everything is possible with you; and, of course, my sons, the best of me.

Is anything as strange as a normal person? . . .
Waiting after school for you, they want to know . . .
If you're normal too
Well, are you?

—Arcade Fire,
"Normal Person"

Somewhere, on the edge of consciousness, there is what I
call a *mythical norm*, which each one of us within our hearts
knows "that is not me."

—Audre Lorde,
Sister Outsider

Contents

Normal
Sucks

— I —

Not Normal

Normalcy was declared. (Normalcy was always a declaration.)
—Arundhati Roy,
The Ministry of Utmost Happiness

Still, it would be progress if we could acknowledge that there really is no such thing as "the normal child": instead, there are *children*, with varying capabilities and varying impediments, all of whom need individualized attention as their capabilities are developed.

—Martha C. Nussbaum,
Frontiers of Justice

Sons,

You have each asked me a question, in different ways, at different times, and, I think, for different reasons. It is the same question I have always feared—but always knew—you would ask me one day.

My oldest, I most clearly remember the night you asked me this question because, of course, you are the oldest and, I admit, I remember your younger years (okay, all your years) more fully than your brothers'. It is one of the many curses of being the oldest. You're forever fixed in my memory, like a frame from a movie, as a child. The night you asked your question, you were five and three-quarters. (You never let me forget those nine months and would yell across a playground, or a parking lot, or the dinner table, if I was asked your age, correcting my rounding down.)

It was bedtime, and I was reading to you from *The Scalawagons of Oz*, an obscure book we'd bought from the used bookstore. Though I was the adult, I stumbled over some of the words. You asked me why. That night I told you for the first time about my dyslexia and my learning challenges. Your response was a single question: "Are you normal, Dad?"

My middle boy, you asked the same question, in a different way, at a different time—but exactly when, I frankly don't remember. As the middle child, the memories of your firsts aren't as linear to me as those of your older brother; the details are blurred around the edges. The sleep deprivation from raising two kids has something to do with it.

You still do things like wake up early and read the *New York Times* sports section cover to cover and solve advanced math problems for fun. You get those tendencies from your mom. But I do remember one morning, likely in the midst of one of your ESPN-worthy rants on the NCAA ranking system, your stopping and asking simply: "Dad, what is normal?"

And then, of course, there's my youngest. You're lucky I remember your name (which I do, even when I call you by your brothers') or your birthday (which I don't, but Mommy does, so we're good). You have a voice like that of a seventy-year-old who smokes a pack a day and an inclination toward the absurd. So I *do* remember the crazy stuff you say, such as "If you didn't have a butt, you couldn't sit down," and the classic, "Chickens are very fast . . . but not in a bicycle race!"

I also remember clearly when you asked me about normal. We were having dinner at a Mexican restaurant near our house, sitting at the bar so we could watch sports. You pointed to three suggestive—okay, completely inappropriate—paintings of women as matadors (because we all know that bull fighting is best done in the nude!) hanging above our seats. You made some hand gestures around your chest that, if you hadn't been six years old and cute, would have gotten us kicked out. "Rocket boobs!" you yelled, as half the bar turned to stare. "Are those *normal?*" you asked, and before I could muzzle you, added, "Why don't Mommy's look like that?"

What is normal? Am I normal? Are you? Are any of us?

When each of you asked, I didn't answer, because I didn't know what to say. I had honestly hoped we would be spared the conversation. That was naive, wasn't it? Because who doesn't, for so many reasons, ask themselves this question at some point, or at many points, in their lives? I did, and I still do, and while I couldn't answer you in the moment, I want to answer you now.

Though you have not been labeled as not normal, as I was, I'm not naive. I know normal will come for you. It will shape you—and it probably already has. We are all up against normal because, as Michel Foucault (who, as you'll quickly discover, I've read way too much of) wrote, "The judges of normality are present everywhere." He didn't stop there: "We are in the society of the teacher-judge, the doctor-judge, the educator-judge, the 'social worker'-judge; it is on them that the universal reign of the normative is based; and each individual, wherever he may find himself, subjects to it his body, his gestures, his behavior, his aptitudes, his achievements." Basically, he's saying we all live in a land governed by these judges' laws, and there's absolutely no getting out of it.

All societies have struggled with normal and, as French anthropologist Claude Lévi-Strauss wrote, we have made the cultural "problem" of differences, anomaly, and abnormality central to every culture. Normal and its twin—*not* normal—are the "fundamental problems of the human condition." We are all surrounded by institutions, systems, and cultural practices that demand and enforce normalcy. We all have to build a life and a self—despite, around, or through—the strict judges of normality's jurisprudence.

I want you to be prepared. I want you to know how to live, and thrive, in a world that will at some point tell you, as it does us all, that you're *not* normal because of what you think, how you look, who you love, how you learn, how you feel, how you behave, or what you believe. I want you to know that normality is a problem to be struggled with, to be resisted, and ultimately, an idea to be rejected and replaced. And I want you to know, if those judges of normality wound you, like they have me and so many others, how to stitch yourself up and fight for a world that is not governed by those judges. When normal comes for you, I want you to be able to say what I couldn't when it came for me. Normal *sucks*.

—

I've been in trouble with normal for a long time. My dilemma started at home. Turn on the bright lights during any performance of familial normalcy and I bet one will find more than a few freak shows. My family is no different. The only difference was that, when I was growing up, my family knew we were strange. We even called ourselves the freak family—Kennedys of a different kind.

I was born in 1977 in San Francisco. Not the San Francisco of today—a bro-tech utopia with sky-high rents—but a dying port town that had seen its last boom and was all bust. California in 1997 wasn't the California I live in today, but a state with half the population it has now, full of escapees from somewhere else—hippies, skaters, surfers, filmmakers, immigrants, oil workers, and everyone else who had been pushed out and sent west. Back then, the state was a radical experiment presided over by Governor "Moon Beam," as the press called him.

My family members were escapees themselves. On both sides, my grandparents were Irish immigrants. My mom's parents landed in New York as children, from County Cork, to be greeted with signs that read IRISH NEED NOT APPLY. They followed those signs all the way to Butte, Montana, a town where the Irish worked copper mines and for a while constituted the largest Irish population outside of Ireland.

My maternal grandmother, Elizabeth, worked as a maid for a prominent Jewish family whom she loved, and they encouraged her to leave Montana as fast as she could. She met my grandfather and did.

My dad's parents saw the same anti-Irish signs but stayed in New York, where they achieved the Irish holy trinity of middle-class respectability by becoming cops, firemen, and politicians. I don't know much about these people. The last time I saw my father's mother I was ten years old and my dad never talked about them. That may have very well been the final time my dad spoke to his mom, but I'm not sure about that either. My dad has a history of dropping out of people's lives, for reasons that took me a long time to understand. I'll get to that later.

My mom was born in San Francisco, but she hasn't told me much about her childhood. I hardly knew my maternal grandmother. I do know she continued to clean rich people's houses until my grandfather became a pharmacist. He died of a heart attack when my mom was ten. My grandmother was a hard woman who had started drinking by lunch, and then after her husband died, by breakfast. My mom was—is—sad, angry, and defiant. She wanted to become a nun, but the church wouldn't allow her in the convent because she was "defiant." She took the hint and decided to become a political radical, joining the Black Panthers, whose headquarters were just a hop, skip, and jump, but a world away, across the bridge in Oakland. According to family legend, she helped break Timothy Leary out of prison.

My mom had my half brother Billy when she was seventeen, my half sister Michelle when she was eighteen and a half, and my half sister Kelly when she was twenty. I came along much later, when she was thirty. We were a ragtag crew. My brother, Billy, looked as if he came right out of central casting for an Irish cop movie, even as a kid; my sister Michelle had long blonde hair and a quiet grace; and my sister Kelly was infamous in our family for what were known as "sit-down strikes," wherein she would just sit down in protest of a perceived childhood injustice, refusing to walk anywhere.

My mom raised my three siblings by herself in a utopian cooperative-housing project called the Squares, which was run by the longshoremen's union. She remembers this time as a kind of paradise in the city, before San Francisco was gentrified, when it was still a place of radical politics and progressive ideas. Less peace and love, more fighting "the Man." The residents of the Squares fought for school desegregation, took control of their local elementary school, and implemented progressive programs. Folks watched each other's kids and shared in each other's lives. My brother and sisters have a different story. In their version, they were left alone a lot and the Squares was a place where children did not have time for childhood. I've learned, as I've gotten older, that both stories can be, and often are, true.

My dad came west slowly, fleeing Tarrytown, New York, in pieces, barely held together by a high IQ, higher education degrees, and a righteous belief in social justice. His father died when he was young, too, and he wasn't told much about what happened. His mom was cold and hard, so his stepdad mostly raised him.

I know that my dad's ears stuck out when he was a kid and his mom taped them to the sides of his head. I know they were devout Catholics and he went to a Catholic school where there was a nun whose nickname was Sister Pain. I know this nickname was well earned. I know that he was injured playing football in high school, crushed at the bottom of a pile of bodies, and doctors fused his lower vertebrae to make him walk "normal." I know my dad never did heal.

I also know that my dad was married before he met my mom, to a woman who I think was named Pamela. Maybe. I'm not sure because Dad never told me. I do know that they had a stillborn child, a son, and then a second child, another half brother. His name is Michael or John (again, I'm not sure) and we have never met. My dad left his son and wife, went west, and didn't look back. He is good at not looking back. I did not know about this half brother until . . . I'm not sure when. My father and I have never talked about him. My half brother's existence has been one of those things that wasn't there and then was—overheard in a late-night argument or slipped in by mistake as my mom catalogued my father's failures over Jack Daniels, neat.

I don't know how my parents met, but I do know that my mom and dad getting married changed the family's economic situation. Kinda. They went from poor and hanging on by their fingernails, to the cusp of the middle-class bell curve. At the time, my father was working for an education company, but he had decided to become a lawyer. He moved the family from San Francisco to Bethesda, Maryland, to attend Georgetown Law School. After law school, he took a corporate law job back in San Francisco, then quit (or was fired—a pattern that would continue for the rest of his life).

I was born on March 19, 1977, at University of San Francisco hospital. Billy was fourteen, Michelle twelve, Kelly ten. While my mom was in labor, they watched *The Mary Tyler Moore Show* in the waiting room and thought up names for me. Michelle offered Tyrone. Kelly countered with Terrell. Billy argued for Stokely, after the leader of the Black Power movement, but also suggested Terrance. I got part of my dad's name, too. My dad is John Gregory Mooney but goes by Greg. I'm Jonathan Terrance Mooney and go by Jonathan. According to my brother and sisters and mom, I'm sure the hell not John.

Less than a year after I was born, my dad declared bankruptcy, and we were evicted from our house. We had to pack up our brown Volvo, named the Incredible Hulk, quickly, before it was repossessed. We left most our belongings on the side of the road but took our dog, Major, and cat, Big Kitty, and pointed the Hulk south, toward Los Angeles, where my dad had a law school buddy and maybe a job.

We landed in Manhattan Beach, California. My folks ran from the wildness of 1970s San Francisco to find middle-class suburbia by the shore. Manhattan Beach was like Lake Wobegon, where everyone was above average—they surfed, lettered in five sports, and were tall and blond. All the kids were the sons and daughters of Boeing executives, doctors, lawyers, accountants. Looking back, I understand why they chose this place; Manhattan Beach was the opposite of the Squares neighborhood in San Francisco. Good schools. Normal people.

Fit in, however, we did not.

I was a weird kid. I was obsessed with checker-patterned clothing, and for a time I rode a checkered bike, wore checkered Vans, checkered shorts, a checkered shirt, and to top it all off, a checkered hat. I loved the television show *Roots* and took to calling myself Kunta Kinte. I would shower only in my socks. I would often run down our hallway naked, yelling, "This is the Democrats on Skid Row!" (I don't get it either.) I decided one year to pee only in the corner of the extra room in our house. No one noticed, which gives you a sense of the general level of cleanliness in our home. I memorized all the dialogue in *Trading Places*—the classic Dan Aykroyd–Eddie Murphy movie about class warfare that was, needless to say, not for children. I had a pretty foul mouth, too. Once, at a doughnut shop, a woman behind the counter asked in the sweetest kid-friendly voice possible how she could help me. I said, "Give me a fucking jelly doughnut, you bitch." I was two.

Our house had no doorknob on the front door, and if you bent down and peeked in through the hole where the knob should have been, you would have gotten a glimpse of the freak show. It was impossible to miss our menagerie of strange animals. Major, the family dog, had a five-inch scar across his face and another on his stomach (no one knew why). Emily was my dog, and she was hairless and skinny, with an opossum's tail. We told ourselves she was a rare African hairless purebred, and I told people she had won the Westminster dog show. My friends said she was a rat. I don't even remember all the cats we had, because at some point we ran out of names and went straight-up literal: Big Kitty, Little Kitty, Orange Kitty, White Kitty, Brown Kitty, Fluffy Kitty, Kitty Kitty, and then . . . Nipper.

Then there was my bird, Charlie. In Manhattan Beach there was a colony of wild parrots that had escaped from a burning pet store, as the urban myth goes. I found Charlie as a baby with a hurt wing on the sidewalk. He had fallen out of his nest and I saved him, took him home, fixed his wing, and loved him. He was the size of a Granny Smith apple, with a green body and yellow-tipped wings and black around his eyes like a prizefighter. He was my best friend. I taught him to talk, and he could say "Hi, John," "Charlie is a pretty bird," and "Fuck you." When I started having a hard time in school, Charlie was often the only one who said hi to me.

My dad walked around naked. A lot. Not only after showers, or on special "Naked Mondays," or nudist holidays, or just on sunny days, but all the time. His drinking started early and ended late. There was a lot of yelling about stuff that I didn't understand. My mom generally was an accomplice in his behavior and failed, like every adult does, in her own ways. But my dad really sucked. He was a figure that loomed over me and rarely talked to me without awkwardness, confusion, anger, or the aid of several Heinekens and a bong hit.

My dad failed in many ordinary ways that I can forgive now, or at least understand and try to forgive. Sometimes I actually do; sometimes I don't. But my dad also sucked in not-so-ordinary ways. In ways that being a fallible human doesn't give him a pass—or at least I don't give him a pass. I did not speak to my dad for more than five years at one point. We never had a falling out, a big blow up, which might be the reason it was so easy, when I was in my midthirties, to let him slip away. The last time I saw him, he looked broken in half. He finally fell off the middle-class part of the bell curve for good, hands bruised and bleeding. But we never talked about it. Not once. So I've filled the silence between me and my dad with only one story—my story—and because it's my story, it's true to me.

I was complicit in the silence as well. I didn't pick up the phone. I didn't look back, either. I guess I'm good at that, too.

It is important to know that despite all this chaos, or maybe even because of it, there was so much good and joy in my childhood. Both my mom and my dad had a deep respect for my siblings' and my voices and believed we should be treated as equal members of the household. We had huge family meetings, that I'm sure were based on some process done in a commune, to collectively decide the rules. ("No walking around naked" was vetoed.) Everyone in the family, in different ways, was encouraged, even required, to challenge authority and question why everything was the way it was. Most important, when it was all said and done, we loved each other.

My childhood was normal to me because I had no reference outside of my own experience. Until one day, I did— and then it wasn't. On that day, I had a playdate with a kid in my neighborhood. My dad was home drinking lentil soup straight from the can, eating a raw head of broccoli and a hard-boiled egg (a normal snack for him), drying his exercise clothes in our oven. He had on a headband, wristbands, sneakers, high white tube socks, and tighty-whities. Our house smelled liked sweat and piss (from me or the animals, I wasn't sure). Charlie, my bird, was cursing up a storm. When the kid from down the street looked around, he puckered up his face and muttered, "*Weird*."

If that wasn't enough, then came school, where I quickly became "one of *those kids*." From my first day in kindergarten at Pennekamp Elementary School, me and school just didn't get along. It started with the desk. My relationship with my school desk was fraught: five seconds into class, my foot starts bouncing; ten seconds in, both feet; fifteen seconds in, I bust out the drums. After a few minutes, it's all over. Then I'm trying to put my leg behind my neck. No, that desk and me did not get along. For some kids, their desk was simply school furniture; for me it was an enhanced interrogation technique that would have made Dick Cheney smile.

Sitting still was hard enough, but I also struggled with reading. I was placed in the "dumb" group. Teachers didn't actually call us the dumb group, but let's be real: everyone knew which group was the "smart" group and which wasn't. My school had the California Condors, the Blackbirds, the Bluebirds—and then over in the annex trailer behind the actual school were the Sparrows. I spent the day reading *See Spot Run*, while the Condors were finishing up *War and Peace*. All joking aside—no matter what the reading groups were named, kids knew their place. *See Spot Run* is not a bad book. Nice narrative structure. Good moral tale. But I didn't want to be caught dead with Spot when I was ten years old. So as I headed across the room to find my reading group, Spot went in my backpack, or under my shirt, because as I walked by, the other kids would taunt: "Jonathan, go back to the dumb reading group."

Reading groups sucked enough, but reading out loud in class was pure hell. Here is how it went for me: first kid starts reading; I'm terrified but have a plan—count the number of sentences this kid is reading, then flip through the book to memorize. Next kid reads. Oh, no. The first kid reads ten sentences; the next kid reads five. I can't find my page. The kid right next to me starts to read. I'm next. I raise my hand. March myself to the bathroom and pray to God I will be skipped when I come back. I come back from the bathroom only to discover that they've waited for me. Held my page. I read out loud for ten agonizing minutes, though *reading* would be an ambitious term for what I did. Fumbling through letters and words would be more accurate.

Then there was writing. I asked my third grade teacher why couldn't there just be one *there*. Do we really need three *theres*? And can't we just agree when I write *how* instead of *who*, or *who* instead of *how*, that he could still get the gist of what I was trying to say? Okay, this *could* be a problem sometimes, like when I passed a note to a kid next to me, intending to ask them *how* they were doing, but instead asking them *who* they were doing. But that is (a) not all that often, (b) funny, and (c) at some point in life a valid question.

Then there were words like *horse* and *house*. Sure, these are totally different things. But give me a break. That *r* in the middle of *horse?* Not my problem. Then words like *organizations* (which often comes out as *orgasm*) and *business* (which I write as *bunnies*) that, due to all those soft consonant vowel blends, can be mangled and rearranged, in endless, beautiful ways. Okay, these words have none of that, or maybe they do. I don't know, because I still don't know what the hell a consonant vowel blend is.

There was a time when we all agreed to just let this stuff go. Sure, that time was the 1500s and spelling wasn't codified, but people got by. One word could be spelled ten ways. Those were the good old days. Pennekamp Elementary School, however, did not believe in the restoration of Old English spelling conventions, so I learned to dumb it down. I would write only with words I could copy from around the room. If the word in my head was too long for me to spell, I used a simpler one. When in doubt, I'd scribble a word so no one could read it. I became caught in a full-blown dumb-it-down cycle. My spelling and writing made me seem stupid, so then I was treated as if I was stupid. Then I began to believe I was stupid, and then I began to act stupid, and then—do it all over again the next day.

———

By the end of third grade I was promoted from being one of "those kids" to the "resource room special ed" kid. I was diagnosed with multiple language-based learning disabilities and attention deficit disorder. When the educational psychologist broke the news to my mom and me, it was as if someone had died. Tissues on the table. Hushed tones. Mirrors covered. We sat shivah for the death of my normality. The tragedy of my problem—which up until that point hadn't had a name—wasn't lost on me, even at ten years old. I knew people thought something was *wrong* with me. When we left the shrink's office, I asked my mom, "Am I normal?"

I can still see my mom that day in my mind. She is a not a tall woman; on a good day, she's four-eleven in high heels, and looks like an Irish bulldog. She has a squeaky voice like Minnie Mouse's and curses like a truck driver. That school physiologist did not want a pissed-off, cursing Minnie Mouse in her office. But that's where my mom went. She asked me to stay outside and then she went back into the office. Next thing I knew, every dog in the neighborhood was running away and I felt as if glass would shatter under the wave of her high-pitched obscenities. She walked out of the office and answered my question with two words: "Normal sucks."

Regardless of what she said, though, I knew the real answer. I had crossed that invisible line between the *normal* and the *not normal*, which we all know is there. Though we aren't quite sure where it is all of the time, or who drew it, or how, or why. At that moment, I knew for sure that whatever normal was, I wasn't it.

———

I want you to know that my story doesn't end outside that office, with me on the wrong side of normal. I want to tell you how I fought my way back, not to the "right" side of the line, but to a sense of self and life that isn't defined by that line at all.

— II —

Normal Hasn't Always Been Normal

The normal was one of a pair. Its opposite was the pathological and for a short time its domain was chiefly medical.
Then it moved into the sphere of—almost everything.

—Ian Hacking,
The Taming of Chance

The normal body, invented in the nineteenth century as a
departure from the ideal body, has shifted over to a new
concept: the normal ideal.

—Lennard J. Davis,
Enforcing Normalcy

When I walked out of that shrink's office with my mom when I was ten, I knew that whatever normal was, I wanted to be it. I am not alone in aspiring to normality, and I don't judge myself, or others, who find themselves on the wrong side of the line and want to get back. I don't judge the people on the right side of the line, either: those who believe they are normal and want to stay there. Because I know, now, that normality is its own kind of rigged carnival game—there are no winners.

We use *normal* without thinking in casual conversation to judge people's actions and behaviors; to draw our own lines of who is in and who is out; to sharpen our individuality and cleave away the "others." We aspire to it in all its ambiguity— *because* of its ambiguity. Ian Hacking summed it up when he wrote that the word *normal*, with its attendant meanings, "whispers in your ear that what is normal is also all right." It's a force like gravity, holding us in place, sorting the fragments and detritus of our world into fixed and knowable categories, so we don't get away from ourselves. It's everywhere-ness is part of its power. It names the world, shapes the world, then justifies to the world its shape with a shrug, *Hey, that's just the way it is.*

But what *is* this thing that I wasn't? No one can be diagnosed, or labeled, as a person with a brain *disorder* or any other *abnormality* without a "normal" to differ from. When I was kid, I really did believe that some very smart scientists must have discovered the normal brain and had it floating in a jar in a laboratory. FYI: they haven't and there wasn't.

You need to know that normal has a history. You may assume that this is a history of discovery—that somewhere, at some point, someone found out what was normal for human beings. And normal, and normal people, are often presented like that—as facts in the world. But that's not true. That is a lie. It's a lie that gives normal such power in our lives. And while normal has a history, it is not a history of discovery, but a history of invention. Normal hasn't always been normal.

—

Where did normal come from, and why does it have the power it does in our lives, in our institutions, in our world? How did it become like air—invisible, essential, all around us? As Ian Hacking was the first to point out, look up *normal* in any English dictionary and the first definition is "usual, regular, common, typical." How did *this* become something to be aspired to? How did everyone being the same achieve the cultural force it has?

There is an entire field of people who study this kind of stuff and have written books about it. *Madness and Civilization* by Michel Foucault is a page-turner. *The Normal and the Pathological* by Georges Canguilhem is laugh-out-loud funny. *Normality: A Critical Genealogy* by Peter Cryle and Elizabeth Stephens should be on your summer vacation reading list. *Enforcing Normalcy* by Lennard J. Davis is a total life changer.

These books, and others, have knocked normal off the pedestal and into the dirt. Because normal *is* contingent—on history, on power, and, most of all, on flawed humans faking it until they make it.

As these scholars have noted, the word *normal* entered the English language in the mid-1840s, followed by *normality* in 1849 and *normalcy* in 1857. This is shocking for a word that masquerades as an ever-present universal truth. When *normal* was first used it had nothing to do with people, or society, or human behavior. *Norm* and *normal* were Latin words used by mathematicians. *Normal* comes from the Latin word *norma*, which refers to a carpenter's square, or T-square. Building off the Latin, *normal* first meant "perpendicular" or "at right angles."

Normal, however, even as a distinct word in geometry, is more complicated than it seems. On the one hand, *normal* is describing a fact in the world—a line may be orthogonal, or normal, or it may not. *Normal* is an objective description of that line. But a right angle, in geometry, is also good, is desirable, is a universal mathematical truth that many mathematicians, then and now, describe as a type of beauty and perfection. Here we see two facets of *normal* that are familiar to us now and make it so powerful. Normal is both a fact in the world and a judgment of what is right. As Hacking wrote, "One can, then, use the word 'normal' to say how things are, but also to say how they ought to be."

A bunch of other words out there were looking to rival *normal*: *natural, common, ordinary, typical, straight, perfect,* and *ideal*. The list goes on. But here's the thing—in the survival of the fittest, *normal* had a key advantage because it could mean more than one thing. Its ambiguity was its strength.

It's scary to think, but it's true: we have *normal* today not because of some deliberate process, or even an organized conspiracy, but because it *worked* better than other words. People started using *normal* in many different contexts and in many different ways because it was there, because it helped them do something, because other people were using it, because it rolled off the tongue, because it gave them power.

So who used *normal*, and why, and how? *Normal* was first used outside a mathematical context in the mid-1800s by a group of men (gender pronoun alert: everyone in this history of normalcy is a man) in the academic disciplines of comparative anatomy and physiology. These two fields, by the nineteenth century, had professional dominion over the human body. It was this crew who first used use the word *normal* outside of a mathematical context, and eventually they used the term "normal state" to describe functioning organs and other systems inside the body. And why did they choose "normal state"? Who the hell knows? Maybe they found the conflation of the factual with the value-driven useful. Maybe there was a professional advantage in appropriating a term associated with mathematical rigor. (At the time, doctors weren't hot shit the way they are now. A doctor's cure for the common cold was leeches; headaches were alleviated by bleeding people, a treatment that killed many, which I guess is a kind of cure; and masturbation was "treated" with castration.) Or maybe they just liked the way it sounded. The historical record is unclear. But use it they did—with great abundance and little rigor—sort of like I do with all words in my ambitious pursuit of creative spelling.

For these guys, "normal state" was used to describe bodies and organs that were "perfect" or "ideal" and also to name certain states as "natural"; and of course, to judge an organ as healthy. I don't blame them for using *normal* instead of *perfect, ideal, natural,* and all the other words they could have used. This wasn't a grand conspiracy. So many words. So little time. I think they just got lazy and said, Screw it, *normal* will do. One word is better than five.

———

The anatomists and physiologists, however, never did find or define the normal state. Instead they studied and defined its opposite—the pathological state. They defined *normal* as what is *not* abnormal. But we absolutely have a proactive definition of *normal* today, don't we?

Normal isn't just *not* abnormal, but it is an upper-middle-class, suburban, straight, able-bodied, and mentally fit married white dude with 2.5 kids. Where did this statistic come from? Well, the 0.5 kid thing gives us an idea of where to start looking. You've never met 0.5 of a child because there is no such thing. The 0.5 children is an abstraction: take all the kids in the country, add them up, divide this by the number of families, and you have an average number of children per household. What is average, however, is often called normal—and what is called normal becomes the norm.

The idea of the average as normal goes back to 1713 to a Swiss mathematician named Jakob Bernoulli, who many consider to be the founder of modern calculus and statistics. He was obsessed with renaissance games of chance (i.e., gambling) and later became obsessed with developing a mathematical equation that would "tame chance" and calculate the odds of random events (i.e., winning or losing in dice). To figure this out, Bernoulli created an equation known as the calculus of probabilities, which became the foundation of all statistics. This was a big deal. The calculus of probabilities specifically, and statistics generally, made many seemingly random events more predictable. With this new way of thinking, Bernoulli challenged and disrupted a deterministic view of the world. He even undermined the Church's whole thing about divine creation and intervention, and perhaps, most important to him, gave people a way to win at craps.

Fast forward a hundred years and the calculus of probabilities gets taken up by Adolphe Quetelet and applied not to gambling but to human beings. Quetelet was the most important European statistical thinker of his time. He was also, as were most of the normalists that came before and after him, ironically, an odd human. He was known to wax poetic about statistical laws and their beauty, and often described finding a mean in a data set in ecstatic terms.

Quetelet was a true believer that statistics should be applied to all aspects of society. He wasn't content to predict which numbered ball would roll out of a slot or how many times heads or tails would come up in a coin toss. In 1835, he put forth the concept of the "average man." His plan was to gather massive amounts of statistical data about any given population and calculate the mean, or most commonly occurring, of various sets of traits—height, weight, eye color—and later, qualities such as intelligence and morality, and use this "average man" as a model for society.

Quetelet was fuzzy on whether he believed that the average man was a real person. On the one hand, he did make many statements about the average man as statistical abstraction. On the other, later in his career, he got more into the idea that there were "types" of humans as a result of a study on the features of Scottish soldiers. (Racism alert: unsurprisingly, he found in this study that black people weren't "normal.") He did make claims that the ideal type could be found in an actual person (though he was thinking of someone like Ewan McGregor). Regardless, Quetelet really believed that "the average man" was perfect and beautiful. The average man was no Homer Simpson—average, as in typical—but rather a model human being who should guide society:

> If the average man were perfectly established, one could consider him as the type of beauty . . . everything that was furthest from resembling his proportions or his manner of being would constitute deformities or illnesses; anything that was so different, not only

in its proportions but its form, as to stand outside the limits observed, would constitute monstrosity.

I find it deeply ironic that even here, in the so-called objectivity of numbers and facts, there lingers the wish for something better than real life. Something greater than ourselves. There is always a dream of self-transcendence, and in that dream, a reality of self-negation. Somewhere, in all of us, we wish to be other than we are.

Quetelet's idea of the average man became the normal man. He used *regular, average,* and *normal* interchangeably. In 1870, in a series of essays on "deformities" in children, he juxtaposed children with disabilities to the *normal* proportions of other human bodies, which he calculated using averages. The normal and the average had merged, as explained in *Normality: A Critical Genealogy*: "The task of statistics was principally to establish just what those normal proportions were, and the job of a therapeutic medical science was to do all that it could to reduce the gap between the actual and the normal/ideal."

But not everyone was feeling what Quetelet was throwing down. He was booed off the stage at many medical symposiums and shunned by the emerging public safety apparatus in France. Often Quetelet's averages weren't representative averages at all. For example, when he calculated the average age of a population, he took out all the kids. When studying what was "natural" for women, he used data from men. It's as if he found that cats are the average pet by averaging only people who had cats. The most damning critique was pretty simple: the average man doesn't exist, by his admission. It is a statistical fiction, so how is the concept of the average man helpful to being a doctor, running a government or school, or living a good life? How is it helpful for anything, really? Because, even according to Quetelet, the average man is the impossible man.

For all Quetelet's talk of the importance of means and averages, and his conflation of the two with normal, he never argued that the average man was a *real* person. He got close with his Scottish "type" thing. And who can blame him? Those accents are rad. But he backed off and argued that the average man was only a useful statistical construct for understanding the world for people in government and other professionals. It wasn't something to actually *be*.

While Quetelet laid the groundwork, no one is more responsible for the modern usage of *normal* than a man named Francis Galton. Galton was Charles Darwin's cousin, began his career as a doctor, and then left medicine for the emerging field of statistics. As Lennard Davis described in his book *Enforcing Normalcy*, Galton made significant changes in statistical theory that created the concept of the norm, as we know it.

While these changes are mathematically complex, here is the CliffsNotes summary: Galton was into the idea of improving the human race and believed that statistics could help. He loved Quetelet's whole "average man" thing but had one minor problem. In the center of Quetelet's bell curve were the most commonly occurring traits, not the ideal bodies and minds Galton believed everyone should have. To solve this problem, Galton, through a complicated and convoluted mathematical process (the technical definition of statistics), took the bell curve idea, where the most common traits clustered in the middle and at the extremes, and created what he called an "ogive" (he had a habit of making up words), which, as Davis explains, "is arranged in quartiles with an ascending curve that features the desired trait as 'higher' than the undesirable deviation." He called this the "normal distribution curve," and it made the most commonly occurring differences that Galton did not value into deficiencies, and the uncommon ideal bodies and minds that he did value . . . *normal*.

This was a big deal. According to Peter Cryle and Elizabeth Stephens, authors of *Normality: A Critical Genealogy*, "Galton was not only the first person to develop a properly statistical theory of the normal . . . but also the first to suggest that it be applied as a practice of social and biological normalization." By the early twentieth century, the concept of a normal man took hold. The emerging field of public health loved it. Schools, with rows of desks and a one-size-fits-all approach to learning, were designed for the mythical middle. The industrial economy needed standardization, which was brought about by the application of averages, standards, and norms to industrial production. Eugenics, an offshoot of genetics created by Galton, was committed to ridding the world of "defectives" (more on this later) and was founded on the concept of the normal distribution curve.

The conflation of the average man as normal was a significant step in the history of normality. Statistics did not discover the normal, but invented the normal as that which *should* occur most often. According to Cryle and Stephens, this was the exact time in history when "a brand of social knowledge grounded in mathematics was asserting that the average mattered more than the exceptions." This was a big deal, especially to those who would later find themselves on the wrong side of normal. As Alain Desrosières, a renowned historian of statistics wrote, with this power play by statistical thought the diversity inherent in living creatures was reduced to an inessential spread of "errors," and the average was held up as the normal—as a literal, moral, and intellectual ideal.

———

Now, one might assume that the history of normal as a history of invention, not discovery, ends here, but it doesn't. Quetelet conceded that the average as normal was a statistical fiction, and Galton did not focus much on normality in a broad sense, but rather on getting rid of those pesky "defectives" on the bottom of the normal distribution curve. It wasn't until the twentieth century that normality became a broad cultural phenomenon, when a new group of professionals picked up the idea of normal, preloaded with all the aforementioned ambiguity, tautology, and conflation with the average, and doubled down on trying to *find* the normal person in the world. Instead, they invented the normal, in all its glory, that is still with us today.

So who were these people seeking out the normal in

human form? Sex scientists. Didn't see that one coming, right? Now, don't get your hopes up. The sex researchers who took normal to new heights were self-described sexual hygienists (try that for pillow talk) and wrote books such as *Rational Sex Ethics: A Physiological and Psychological Study of the Sex Lives of Normal Men and Women, with Suggestions for a Rational Sex Hygiene with Reference to Actual Case Histories.* *Fifty Shades of Grey* this is not. But people started paying attention to these sex scientists, because, no matter what, sex sells.

According to Cryle and Stephens, along with these researchers studying sex, psychologists, psychiatrists, sexologists, psychoanalysts, public health officials, and marital advice writers led a broad and popular movement in the twentieth century to find the normal and tell us all about it. The informal leader of this whole crew, of course, was Sigmund Freud. Yes, the man with a cocaine habit that would have killed a small farm animal was one of the most important thinkers in the history of normality. I'll skip the long dissertation on Freud and spare you the pain of reading his tomes. Bottom line: it's all about sex. All of it. Everything. One's whole personality, thoughts, aspirations, hopes in the world, favorite color, food, flavor of ice cream, whatever—all of it comes down to sex.

In the late nineteenth and early twentieth centuries, Freud and others developed theories of normal sexuality, and by default, because sexuality was everything, the normal person. At first, they fell into the old "normal as what is *not* normal" tautology and focused almost entirely on "deviance." The first major book on this subject was *Psychopathia Sexualis* (that's Latin for freaky sex stuff), written by Richard von Krafft-Ebing. He was a true jerk, and I could disparage him for so many reasons, at the top of the list that he was among the first to declare that people who had encounters with the same sex were sick and deviant and should go to jail. Freud, though, flipped this on its head. He asserted that there wasn't a clear line between normal and abnormal. Instead, everyone was a little "perverted" and "sick." This was a big idea that others, beginning in the 1920s, popularized in the marriage and self-help (yes, *that* kind of self-help) literature of the day as being "nearly normal."

Nearly normal is an interesting and useful (for some) but ultimately maddening new layer to the hot mess of normality. It was a great business model for shrinks, because if everyone is a little sick, then everyone could use their services. The publishing business loved it, because advice manuals could help the nearly normal get closer to normal. And the exploding mass-market consumer economy and the advertising industry seized on the idea, too, because if you want to sell something to someone, tell them something is wrong with them and you've got the thing to fix it.

But what the hell does it mean to be nearly normal? This makes my head spin: there is a normal, but I'm not it. However, I shouldn't accept this fact, but instead strive for a normality that no one can be. And, oh yeah, here are a bunch of things you can buy, and people you can pay, to help you overcome your near-normality disorder. I can see why Freud needed all that cocaine.

In this way, normal was now not just a thing to be but a thing to become. But wait. I have good news. At the same time the shrinks were pontificating about normality, and our lack thereof, another group was hard at work finding a way to untie this Gordian knot of contradictions. A new generation of "sexual hygiene" researchers—think a cross between a PE and sex ed teacher—took the study of normality to a new level. In 1930, after almost a hundred years of normal slowly creeping into more and more aspects of our lives, the first large-scale study of the normal person occurred: the Grant Study of Normal Young Men at Harvard. What? Is that right? Normal young men at *Harvard*?

Yes, the first study of normal people ever done was a study of white men at a university that, at the time, admitted no one but white men. The study was directed by Arlie V. Bock, professor of hygiene. The team of researchers collected a broad range of physiological, social, and psychological data and . . . Forget it. Let's get to the point. Because I think we all know what they found. The study found—drum roll please—that rich, college-educated white men are normal.

According to the study, the normal person was a "balanced harmonious blending of functions that produce good integration." Translation: the *normal* men of this study were normal because they were successful in a system that was dominated by men just like them. You are normal if your behavior, appearance, and background *are* the dominant culture. You are normal if you fit into this culture and are therefore deemed normal by the school, the church, the town, the doctor, the professor. Normal is what works in society's norms. This is a whole new tautology—normal is what is called normal by people who are considered normal.

———

What a mess the twentieth century made out of normal. The sex researchers and Harvard demographers took a perfectly good dichotomy of normal and not normal and muddied it all up, and now the concepts were all over the place. I wish I could say people just threw up their hands in revolt and gave up on the whole idea. But we know that's not true. This normal became all things, to all people, and so it became, truly, everything.

By midcentury this new normal was set in stone. Literally. I mean they actually made stone statues of normal. If you are ever in Cleveland, you *have* to go to the Museum of Natural History, where down in the basement you will find two statues called Normman and Norma, which were produced in 1945 as representations of the normal man and woman. These statues were intended to be the most realistic and data-driven representations of normality ever made. These were not like the statue of David, an embodiment of the ideal human, which no one could actually be, but models of the normal human based on biometric data from hundreds of thousands of people.

To create Norma, as Cryle and Stephens wrote, researchers used a data set that averaged measurements taken of white

American women, "recorded and standardized by the Bureau of Home Economics in the 1940s in an attempt to devise the first standardized system of sizing for ready-made clothes" (this gave us the generic medium for clothing, i.e., the mean size).

Normman was modeled on data collected by Charles Davenport at the Cold Spring Harbor Laboratory. Davenport was a card-carrying eugenicist (more on him, and *that*, later). To quote Cryle and Stephens, with some *minor* commentary of my own interjected, "The data used to create Normman drew from Davenport's vast collection of World War I soldiers' body measurements" (white dudes), "augmented by records from a body measurement laboratory set up at the Chicago World's Fair in 1933" (more white dudes) and "insurance company data" (white dudes again), "as well as results from surveys of male college students undertaken by physical anthropologists working in university contexts" (even more white dudes). This means, if you are counting, that this data was 150 percent white dudes, bringing the total number of white dudes to a staggering, NASCAR-friendly, Connecticut-country-club, if-they-all-laid-down-you-would-think-it-snowed number of white dudes.

Norma and Normman first went on display at the Museum of Natural History in New York in June 1945, to rave reviews. Norma and Normman were such big hits that the Cleveland Museum of Health bought the statues and held a competition to find the living embodiment of Norma. Right off the bat, everyone clearly could tell who was *not* normal:

anyone else who wasn't the color of porcelain, people with physical differences of any sort, and LGBTQ people, because Normman and Norma were presented as a heterosexual couple ready to get it on for the good of the nuclear family.

The competition ran for ten days and was launched with a front-page article in the *Cleveland Plain Dealer* titled "Are you Norma, typical woman?" As Peter Cryle and Elizabeth Stephens rightly note, the irony of this timing is telling. It's 1945. The United States has nuked Japan. German death camps have been liberated. Europe is in ruins. And for ten days, the fourth-largest newspaper in the country ran front-page stories about normality.

More than 3,700 women sent in their measurements. On September 21, 1945, finalists were invited to an open house held at the Cleveland YMCA. More than a thousand people came to watch the finalists be measured by the judges of normality. The winner was Martha Skidmore, a cashier at a local movie theater. Nice lady. Finally, after one hundred years of debate, someone had found the normal. Praise Jesus. Make her queen.

From the podium the judges rose to crown Martha as normal. With a smile on his face, the Ohio commissioner of mental hygiene and physical health looked at Martha, then looked at Norma, then looked out at the crowd and said that the living embodiment of Norma had been found . . . kinda. The only problem was, as a reporter for the *Cleveland Plain Dealer* wrote, "Martha's measurements did *not* coincide with those of the statue. . . . After assessment of the measurements of 3,863 women who entered the search, Norma remains a hypothetical individual."

Sorry, Martha. Sorry, me. Sorry, other humans. Tough break. The judges of normality have spoken: There *is* a normal. It's an impossible thing to be. So don't stop trying to be it.

———

If you're confused by this history, then you're paying attention. This history shows how normal became the normal we live with now: a mash-up of the standard, average, perfect, ideal. Not as something to aspire to, but as something to be. A constantly shifting, expanding horizon we are told to chase.

I wanted you to know this history because it is a history of our present. There is no place in your life, now or ever, where you won't encounter normal as an impossible ideal you're supposed to embody. We live in a world of norms that will be used to rank and judge our intelligence, health, height, weight, desires, love, and ultimately our value. But normal has never been objectively true, nor has it ever objectively quantified what is good or right in us.

Normal was created, not discovered, by flawed, eccentric, self-interested, racist, ableist, homophobic, sexist humans. Normal is a statistical fiction, nothing less. Knowing this is the first step toward reclaiming your power to define yourself, know yourself, and love yourself for who you are, not who you should be.

— III —

Abnormal

ab·nor·mal
adjective: deviating from what is normal or usual, typically in a way that is undesirable.

ab·nor·mal·i·ty
noun: an abnormal feature, characteristic, or occurrence, typically in a medical context.

Since almost everyone tries to appear as "normal" as possible, those who appear clearly "abnormal" according to their society's standards are constant reminders to those who are currently measuring up that they might slip outside the standards.

—Susan Wendell,
The Rejected Body

As I was writing this to you, a speech I gave about my struggles in school and challenges with normal was posted on Facebook and went viral—the video was watched more than nineteen million times. I have to admit, I was overwhelmed by this response. A part of me figured that my story must be getting old, as I am, which you, as my children, so kindly point out pretty much every day.

We live in the golden age of diversity, right? I figure if we are all special now, my school experiences, which happened decades ago, would at some point be obsolete; that they were simply a dispatch from the bad old days of the 1980s, a time long ago when everyone listened to Def Leppard and wore stone-washed jeans, when rattails were cool and kids were sorted into "smart" and "stupid" reading groups, and normal reigned supreme.

Well, that was naive, wasn't it?

Every day, in every community, all around the world, people with differences are demeaned. Just look at the data. According to multiple research studies, including the UN World Report on disability, people with cognitive and physical differences have the worst life outcomes, as measured by employment, wages, and education achievement, of any minority group in the world. I know this personally because of my own experiences, but also from the tens of thousands of stories of shame, marginalization, and dehumanization that I have read or listened to directly.

These stories are all different and all the same. Whether it is autism, cerebral palsy, deafness, visual impairments, dyslexia, depression, ADHD, and everything in between, there is a common experience of differences being treated as abnormality and deficiency—in school and at work, as well as in families and communities. Because of this way of relating to, understanding, and ultimately treating differences, humans with these differences are dehumanized, victimized, and wounded.

After the Facebook video of my speech was posted, I received more emails and messages than at any point during my twenty years of advocacy. Here is one message, of the thousands, that I got from a boy named Elliot in the United Kingdom:

> I'm Elliot i live in England and I'm 9,. mum let me rite too you I hope that's ok. I watched your video (mum said no but I watched it) and it made me sad and happy. Because I just found out I'm severely dyslexic and I'm in year 4 at school and I thought I would never be able to do anything because I'm just so rubbish at school and everyone is so much better than me at everything really and I always come last at everything even when i really try, and it makes me so sad. art and computer that is the only thing in the world that i can do. But I can't read hardly any books because i get mixed up. I told my teacher I want to be a writer because I like to write stories on my

computer about an imaginary land full of funny Big and small creates and things, but she said im not good at spelling, she is actually totally right . . . Mum says I'm not rubbish at everything but mums always says nice things I think so I donet actually believe her all the time. ;-) I'm rubbish

I am waiting for school to finish forever (in 7 years I think) so I never ever ever have to read or learn anything again and I hate it there . . . What age you was when you wrote the book, did someone check your spellings in the book and did everyone stop being mean to you when you wrote it? Donet worry if your to busy to replay I understand you must have a lot of thing to do. From eillot age 9

How the hell do we still have a world where a kid like Elliot, who clearly has so much good in him, feels like human garbage? I've spent my life trying to understand how we've gotten to this place where natural variation in human beings—variation that brings with it strengths and weaknesses, ability and disability, good and bad—is understood as pathology.

The answer, of course, is that normal needs the Elliots of the world to be on the bottom. Normal has always been propped up by and constructed on the bodies and lives of the not normal. And to be on the bottom of that pile, to be the negation of normal that is its foundation, is to not just differ from normal; it is to be normal's opposite—abnormal—which is false and wrong.

45

Just because normal isn't a fact doesn't mean it hasn't been used to dehumanize people with differences. But it doesn't have to be this way. Like normal, abnormal has a history, not of discovery but of invention. As you make your life, you need to know this history and the process and systems of normalization that have turned natural differences among humans into abnormalities to be diagnosed, categorized, and then of course, corrected. You are round pegs, as we all are, and no matter how much I try, I can't protect you from the relentless message that you must fit the square hole.

———

A few days after I was officially diagnosed, at the end of third grade, my mom and I went to breakfast at Uncle Bill's Pancake House in Manhattan Beach. This was the place we went when I needed to ditch school and feel better. That morning at breakfast my mom and I read the report from the school psychologist about my learning problems.

Spoiler alert: there wasn't much good news in that document. I knew the moment I walked out of that shrink's office that even though she said there were no right answers (always bullshit, by the way), I had bombed the tests I was given. Sure, there were some parts of the assessment that I thought I had crushed. I had nailed the block building test, for sure. I thought I had done okay on the whole inkblot thing. For the first inkblot, I'd told her that it looked like a school on fire. The second inkblot, like a teacher on fire; the third inkblot looked like her—I had paused for dramatic effect—on fire. I'd waited for her to laugh. She did not.

It was all downhill after that. I bombed a test where I was asked to remember a string of numbers while various noises were made at random times to distract me, which frankly just seemed mean. I asked her if she wanted to know about the bird's nest outside the office window. She said no. Handwriting and spelling, of course, were a shit show, because we all know that when you don't know how to spell a word you scribble it so no one can tell. Reading was the straw that broke the shrink's back. I told her that I could read with my eyes closed, which is true, because I was good at memorizing things that had been read to me. She was not impressed. That, she said, was not reading, to which I replied, "Says who?"

Over chocolate-chip-blueberry pancakes with whipped cream and extra syrup (it was one of those days), I watched my mom try to make sense of this report. I can only imagine what it felt like to have her child described to her by people who did not know me at all, in language that was inherently negative. She read a lot of it out loud—though I don't think she meant to—because she was overcome with anger. "Jonathan has language processing—*what the fuck*—disorder." "Jonathan has extreme deficits of phonetic—*which isn't even a goddamn word*—awareness." "Jonathan has extreme—*who the fuck do they think they are*—dis-inhibition and self-regulation deficits." "Jonathan displays poor executive—*my god, I'll kill them*—function." This went on for about ten minutes until the restaurant manager politely asked us to leave.

My mom did her best that morning, and during the rest of my life, to resist my being pathologized. Difficult children, she often said, make interesting adults. Nonconformity is strength. Just look at how Timothy Leary turned out, and he had *reading problems*. All the Black Panthers she knew had learning differences (super helpful to hear if you are a white kid from the suburbs). And, of course, her go-to favorite: nothing was wrong with me, I was just a late bloomer. She had said this before and would say it again and again. She had stolen the line from *Leo the Late Bloomer*, a kid's book about a lion who can't do things like the other animals. Leo can't read. He can't write. He can't eat nicely. But despite these challenges, Leo blooms. My mom read this book to me until I was eighteen years old.

The pancakes and her anger at the school were nice and all, but I knew the truth: I wasn't different, as my mom said. I was deficient. I never did read the whole report, but I didn't need to. I got it. I had brain disorders. I wasn't just *not* normal, which I could have lived with; I was *abnormal*. Somehow I knew this was—though I wasn't quite sure why at the time—a whole different ball game.

———

What does it mean to become an *abnormal* human? What does it mean to be a problem? How does it feel? A philosopher I admire named Ron Mallon believes that the categories used to classify people, such as race, gender, ability, disability, can be made up or invented and yet real, both "causally significant" and "scientifically meaningful" at the same time. They may be invented, but these made-up categories still affect people. There can be a looping effect where the person and the "problem" merge, reflecting back each to itself, until the two are inseparable.

Technically, an abnormality is something (or someone) that is uncommon or atypical. But we all know that to label something an abnormality is absolutely negative. The world *abnormality* comes directly from disease-based medical professions as a description of something/someone that is *unhealthy*. According to the Oxford English Dictionary, an abnormality is an abnormal feature, characteristic, or occurrence, typically in a *medical* context.

The sorting of typical humans into hierarchical medical categories of difference was not inevitable. Human differences had been, before this sorting, interrupted in other ways. Charles Darwin proved that all evolution was fueled by variation. Before the category of the abnormal, people with cognitive and physical differences were often considered wonderful, eccentric, remarkable, singular, extraordinary, queer, odd, strange, whimsical, absurd, and curious. According to Henri-Jacques Stiker, a disability historian, people with cognitive and physical differences during the Middle Ages "were spontaneously part of a world and of a society that was accepted as being multifaceted."

What changed?

Difference became abnormality when the probability

theorists, skull counters, and shrinks who brought us normal become coconspirators with the great sorters of the early twentieth century. Normal emerged, side by side and arm in arm, with the rise of science as a tool to describe and make sense out of the world. During the eighteenth and nineteenth centuries, biologists created systems to categorize the natural world, astronomers mapped the sky, geographers the world, and anatomists the human body. Normal lurked in the background, drawing a line in these charts and systems between what was acceptable and what was not—and we all know that the *not* is abnormal.

Normal and abnormal came directly out of the late-nineteenth and early-twentieth-century practices of measuring bodies (and later brains) called anthropometrics. Anthropometry involves the systematic measurement of the physical properties of the human body, mostly descriptions of body size and shape. It was an early tool of anthropology used for the purposes of understanding human variation. We've already met some of the pioneers of anthropometrics in the history of normal. Quetelet's whole "average man" idea came out of anthropometric measuring, and Norma and Norm-man were created using a wide variety of anthropometric data gathered in the mid-twentieth century. There are also others, like Francis Galton, who invented psychometrics, a branch of anthropometrics, which focuses on measuring more subjective cognitive traits such as intellect, personality, mental ability, and character.

Here's the thing: As we saw with the idea of the "average

man," anthropometric and psychometric measurement was never just about gathering data, creating a category, and leaving it at that. The statistical act of measuring humans led to the creation of the normal distribution curve, where the center of the curve was good, and variation from the center was bad. This dichotomy spread throughout the scientific community during the twentieth century like a viral Facebook cat video. Diverse scientific fields, including anthropology, medicine, and then the emerging disciplines of psychology and psychiatry, began to describe human variations from the norm as *abnormalities*. As disability rights activists and scholars Sharon L. Snyder and David T. Mitchell have argued, this was not an "objective" science of human variability, but a judgmental science that categorized and ranked some humans as biologically better than others.

It was the physical anthropologists who pioneered anthropometric measurement. These white guys (of course) focused on measuring people's skulls, a practice called craniometry. They collected thousands of skulls from graves all over Europe, in addition to subjecting thousands of people to tedious head-measuring sessions. What were they looking for? From the beginning, they set out to find "racial" types. Take the work of Paul Broca, one of the founders and leaders of physical anthropology, as a prime example. As he collected and measured skulls, he omitted "deformed" individuals, children, and people of different non-white races from his studies. He did this because if these populations were to be included "one would then be committing a grave error in considering all men as if they made a single group. That would mean giving up on the search for the craniological characters of the different races." In other words, he decided there were different races before he even started and then, *surprise*, discovered that skull sizes proved there were different races. This selection bias led to the separation of humans into groups and to the exclusion of atypical individuals from the normal range for each group. Just take a wild guess which groups he, and most of the other physical anthropologists, concluded were superior. Rich, educated, able-bodied white guys.

In the 1850s, a field emerged in Italy known as criminal anthropology, which was committed to discovering, through a wide variety of measurements, the "socially dangerous individual" as both a class and a race. The leader of this movement was Cesare Lombroso, who analyzed everything from jaw size to nose shape to hair loss. He concluded that "many of the characters present in savage men and colored races often recur in born criminals." In case you are interested, none of his measurements have any link whatsoever to criminality.

As if labeling groups of human beings "natural born criminals" wasn't bad enough, along came psychometrics. This "science"—here the quotes are absolutely warranted— focused on quantifying and measuring internal subjective states such as intelligence, personality, and character. The founder of this group was Francis Galton, whom I will discuss in greater detail later because inventing psychometrics is the *least* interesting/scary thing about this guy. What you need to know now is that he was Charles Darwin's cousin and was inspired by Darwin's studies of variations in animals to attempt the same in humans.

Galton wasn't the first to measure humans, but he did, as Cryle and Stephens wrote, "dramatically expand the range of both what could be measured and who should be measured." He worked with schools to measure students' vision and hearing. He had families throughout the United Kingdom measure themselves daily. He was the first to develop mental tests including reaction time, visual acuity, and verbal ability; and he was the first to study "intelligence" in a research project on "hereditary genius." Galton's goal with all this measuring? In his words: "Grade physically and mentally (all) of mankind." Just guess which groups got Fs? Us abnormal ones.

This new science of measuring, grading—and therefore judging—humans, as I'm sure you've noticed, did not just create a hierarchy but also *pathologized* the people in these ranked categories. To pathologize is to label a trait a sickness or a disease. With the introduction of this concept, abnormality became colonized by the medical profession in the mid-nineteenth century. At this time doctors were emerging from the bad old days of leeches and lancets to greater social prominence, due in part to the fact that scientists had discovered the physical origins of some diseases and doctors had gotten better at actually saving lives rather than killing people.

From the nineteenth century up until today, the medical

profession has used the prevention of disease and the control of the abnormal as a source of professional power. This is specifically true with "mental medicine." In the mid-to-late 1800s, modern psychiatry was born, and it focuses on human behavior, with its deviation and abnormality. At this time there is an expansion of categories, called "syndromes," for eccentricities like agoraphobia, claustrophobia, kleptomania, exhibitionism, introversion, and masochism. It is also the first time that homosexuality appears as a pathological syndrome, i.e., a sickness, in psychiatric literature.

The mash-up, in the late nineteenth and early twentieth centuries, of normal/abnormal with the medical idea of healthy/unhealthy was used to discount entire populations as biologically inferior. Whole groups of humans would now find themselves as members of a pathologized category; for example, in 1904 students struggling in French schools (kids like me, but with cooler accents) were called in an official state report "physically, intellectually, and morally *abnormal* children." Homosexuality, which has been around for as long as humans have been sneaking off into the bushes, was declared a "perversion" and outlawed throughout Europe. Black people were labeled and classified as "subhuman," and slaves who ran away from slavery were diagnosed as having "drapetomania" (an actual clinical diagnosis at the time that translates to "runaway slave madness"). Women were "scientifically proven" to be biologically inferior to men (in fairness, the normalizers got this one from the Bible). People historically considered slow, or simple, were reclassified as feebleminded and defective, and were incarcerated around the world.

This is a long list that just keeps going and becomes quite redundant. Pretty much anyone who deviated from the middle of the bell curve was categorized as sick and less than. Differences became abnormalities. Normal was used to create dehumanizing categories of social disqualification, based on a narrow continuum of acceptable human variation—the grand total of which was none. This biologically based, scientifically justified discrimination disqualified a wide range of humans and had a huge impact on atypical bodies and minds. Variability becomes disability, abnormality, and pathology. From here on, this medical model will become the foundation for how society makes sense of, addresses, and treats cognitive and physical differences. The medical model makes variability synonymous with sickness and puts the social "problem" to be solved *in* the person, not the environment *around* the person.

The great sorting and pathologizing of difference are still with us today. This is dangerous, because if there is one thing I know, really know to my core, it's that to define deviations from the norm as a deficit or disorder or abnormality is the first step in making a person into a problem to be fixed and a sickness to be cured. Because while *Leo the Late Bloomer* is a book that I love, I knew the truth: Leo would have been screwed if he'd been in Ms. G's class.

Room 503, Pennekamp Elementary School, was called a lot of things: the 'tard room, the SPED room, the short bus dock, the resource room, and the special room. My teacher was named Ms. G. She loomed over me, a towering figure of authority, and I saw her as faceless, without a history, hopes, or dreams. I'm sure, in reality, she was thirty-five, had a family, or a dog, and was confused most of the time, like most of us are. Fake it until you make it, Ms. G.

My first day in her class, she sat me down and did an evaluation for my individual education plan, or IEP, a document students in special education settings often have. The IEP would be a tool to organize my learning. But make no mistake about it—this document is a surveillance file. The KGB and NSA have got nothing on the IEP. Here is what went into my file: *hyperactive with moments of inattentiveness, poor handwriting, below grade level in phonic awareness, consonant blending and spelling, executive function deficits, organizational challenges, speech problems.*

What about the rest of me?

After we talked, I met the others kids in room 503. We didn't make eye contact. Some were new to the class, like me. Some weren't. They all had files like mine, different in the deviations from the norm and in what interventions would be required, but in that, we were the same. I had seen these kids around school and knew them. Steven had a buzz cut with a rattail and was so desperate to be successful, he tried to copy *my* work. Mary cried a lot and swore she could feel colors. Ben couldn't feel most of his body because of something the teachers called CP and when he spoke he sounded as if he was sucking a straw. I thought his brain was broken. And then there was Julio. He, everyone knew, was just bad. I'm ashamed to admit that I had called many of these kids retards. Short-bus riders. Spazzes. Freaks. Stupid. Idiots. Dummies. But now I was one of them, so I called myself these names; as many of us did, out of defiance, to beat others to the punch, and because we knew it was true.

That room, that file, Ms. G, the practices and policies that sort people into types of humans and gather up the ones who don't fit, didn't come from nowhere. That great sorting of humans is not in the past, but stuck right here in our present, like shards of glass that refract, reflect, and puncture our day to day—and wound some of us deeply. Ms. G and all the others who put me in that classroom were not bad people. It would be easier if they were; it would make it hurt less if there was a villain. But this is a crime of good intentions. It's a crime committed by people who care about others, each doing a job in an institution and a system that came from a *somewhere* that is still here today.

———

Michel Foucault called the cultural systems and institutions that pathologize and seek to remediate differences the "normalizing society." I know you might be sick of hearing this guy's name, but in my quest to understand the social power of normality, Foucault is like a background cowbell in a Blue

Öyster Cult song: you can never have enough. Foucault has done more than any other scholar to show the corrosive cultural power of normality. In his book *Discipline and Punishment* (it's a light read), Foucault documented the emergence of normal as a form of power that took control of "life itself." Every society has made claims to the body—obligations, restrictions, and interventions—but the claims and demands on people in the normalizing society are different. Social theorist Nikolas Rose calls this biopolitics, a new form of social power that is "concerned with our growing capacities to control, manage, engineer, reshape, and modulate the very vital capacities of human beings as living creatures." As Ann Waldschmidt, a sociologist and disability theorist, wrote in her groundbreaking essay "Who Is Normal? Who Is Deviant?": "The central means of social control in normalization society is the statistically backed comparative description of people, their behavior, and their characteristics." This type of society is organized to make us more alike than different.

The normalizing society uses the statistical abstraction of normal as its organizing principle. Schools, factories, cities, towns, and even families are designed and built, not for the reality of differences, but on the dream that we could, and should, all somehow, someday be the same. Schools are designed for the middle of the bell curve. The nuclear heterosexual family is solidified as normal; and architecture, city planning, industrial production, and product design adopt Norma/Normman-like body ideals to shape our environment.

As Foucault documented, in school and work, human

beings are judged by categories that did not exist before: intelligence, attention, inattention, lateness, absences, interruption of tasks, negligence, lack of zeal, impoliteness, disobedience, idle chatter, irregular gestures, lack of cleanliness—all these are new judgments for human behavior based on an idea of normal. Each category is tracked, organized, and enforced through new systems of quantification and control, such as the timetable, rows of school desks, charts, mathematical tables, ranked groups, files, and mass consumer marketing.

In the normalizing society, those of us who can't learn to be, or at least appear to be, normal are targeted for rehabilitation. The historian Henri-Jacques Stiker has described how, after World War I, there was an explosion of institutions, government systems, and private-sector products dedicated to restoring the "abnormal" to an "assumed prior normal state." Here the dream of the same became an enforced reality for the different. Medical interventions proliferated to correct atypical bodies and minds; new pedagogical approaches for the "feebleminded" and others were invented. The French and US governments created departments of "rehabilitation" in the early twentieth century. In 1975, in the United Kingdom, France, and the United States, special education was born.

———

I want to be clear: special ed was not a nefarious plot that was hatched, in a staff room over bad coffee, by middle-aged teachers like Ms. G to enforce normalcy. Special education's invention was progress. For much of human history, people with brain and body differences were denied education and thought to be incapable of learning. According to a report from the National Council on Disability, before the passage of federal special education laws, many states had laws that explicitly excluded children with certain types of disabilities, including children who were blind or deaf and children labeled "emotionally disturbed" or "mentally retarded." In 1919, for example, the Wisconsin Supreme Court ruled in *Beattie v. Board of Education of City of Antigo* that students with physical impairments could be excluded from school if their presence was deemed depressing or nauseating to other students. According to the same report, even by the late 1970s, "schools in America educated only one in five students with disabilities. More than 1 million students were excluded from public school and another 3.5 million did not receive services."

Special education was, and still is, a bold idea that challenged deeply held beliefs about which humans had capacities to learn and grow. The approach, experience, and goal of special education, however, can be traced back to the historical moment when normal/abnormal was used to categorize groups of human beings as inferior. Special education, to quote a prominent thinker of the time, "should be a sieve through which those who will not be self-supporting, those who will not be law-abiding, and those who will not have proper supervision shall not pass unless to enter a custodial institution. Provision should be made to study these children and to secure their admission to an institution for defectives before they leave school to go to work." While special education has its origins in segregating and warehousing the abnormal, by the 1950s it became committed to "correcting" people with disabilities. Post–World War II, a culture of normality fueled a remediation industrial complex that sought to "fix" and "cure," as opposed to accommodating, people with differences.

The purpose of these systems of rehabilitation, like special education, was never to build a true, helpful world around the reality of difference. Nope. "Readjustment," Stiker wrote, "must be to society, as society is presently constituted." The purpose of these systems was always to normalize, to make the round peg fit the square hole.

———

In room 503, once I was one of those kids with a file, I became a person to be corrected. The list of things to be corrected included my handwriting—without question the most important skill for success in the modern world. My experience with handwriting correction followed the best practices from special education textbooks. First, there was the correction of my body positioning. A distance of two fingers must be left between my body and the table, both feet flat on the floor, paper at a 45-degree angle toward the writing-arm side, hold the pen or pencil close to the writing tip with the thumb and index fingers, the middle finger should be curved under the writing utensil with the utensil resting lightly on the area between the tip and first knuckle, the fourth finger and pinkie should be curved in toward the palm.

Then came the letters. As outlined in countless handwriting instructional manuals, similarly shaped letters should be the same height. For example, small letters (*a, c, e, i, m, n, o, r, s, u, v, w, x, z*) should be half the size of ascenders (*b, d, h, k, l, t*) and descenders (*g, j, p, q, y*). Capital letters should be about the same height as ascenders. The space between each letter in a word should be the same. The space between each word also should be consistent. I used my pinkies to measure the correct distance between words. I practiced letters by tracing each letter of the alphabet with my finger. Then if I was working with a progressive teacher, up-to-date on the most recent innovation in tactical kinetic learning, I traced the letters with my tongue. All of this took up about forty-five minutes of my day and provided ample time for the teacher to do reports on her computer.

I haven't told many people before, but I had a speech impediment. What this impediment was, I'm still not sure. I know that even now I'm constantly asked where I'm from and if I'm European. But that happens mostly in the Midwest. I rolled my *R*s, which made me sound as if I was born in South Boston and raised in Brooklyn by an itinerant band of surfers. I thought it was cool. It required drastic intervention. I was told to hold out my tongue. It was adjusted. I stood in front of a mirror and said, "Red rover, red rover, in a field of clover, come on over," a bunch of times. Did this work? I'm still often asked if I'm from New Zealand.

B. F. Skinner was the patron saint of many of the schools I attended. Operant conditioning, a form of behavioral modification that behaviorists first employed on pigeons, was the preferred method of crowd control. When I was in school, special education might as well have been one big sticker chart, driven by a premodern token economy. Walk in the classroom quietly, get a token, start working right away, get a token, raise your hand, get a token, sit still, get a token, clean your desk, get a token. Say please and thank you, get a token. Express an original thought. No token. And then there was the gold star behavior chart. Steven was at the top with twenty gold stars. Sally had fifteen. Jacob had ten, and then I had a hundred stars, but all of my stars were black.

Next comes phonic instruction. For phonics, as outlined in a popular reading program, there is a set of index cards with individual letters on them. The teacher shows me a card and says "This letter says /eee/. Say it with me." I say /eee/ with the teacher. She says, "Now you say it." I say /eee/. Trust me, this was as fun as it sounds.

After the cards, the teacher tells me that I will hear two words that have only one sound that is different. My job is to identify the sound that is different: the beginning, middle, or ending sound. The teacher says *cat/fat, map/mop, rap/rat*. I say they rhyme. Wrong. I say that the cat can use the mop to de-map the fat rat. Wrong. She tells me to identify the position in which the discriminating phoneme is found.

I ask her to stop speaking Latin.

She says to me, "Listen, my lion puppet likes to say the sounds in words. The sounds in *mom* are /mmm/-/ooo/-/mmm/. Say the sounds in *mom* with us."

I ask her what she's been smoking.

———

My parents, and many teachers, did the best they could to resist my correction. In elementary school, every Friday was spelling test day. What an awesome way to end the week! Every day leading up to spelling test day was spelling remediation day. What a fun way to spend the week. Monday was flash cards; Tuesday was drawing the words in the sand; Wednesday was building the words with blocks; Thursday was doing interpretive dance about the words; Friday was always failing the spelling test.

One Friday, however, I came down to the breakfast table as usual, but there were no flash cards or blocks or any other form of last-minute cramming with my Pop-Tarts. That day my mom and I ditched school and went to the zoo. After that first Friday, we did that almost every Friday, for as long as I can remember. I'm alive today in part because of those Fridays.

My dad, too, did his best, which wasn't all that great, but it was something. My dad had a harder time resisting than my mom. Out of nowhere, the culture of correction would get him again, and he often yelled at me to buck up and work harder, or threatened that I would be a high school dropout. He had changed, hadn't he? So I should change, too.

I get it now. All those PhDs, MDs, assessments tests, and textbooks with big scientific words telling you that your kid is wrong, broken, and defective, and then telling you that your job is to fix them: that's hard to resist. It's a perfect storm of scientific objectivity.

Many of my teachers were lost in the storm as well. But not all of them. One day in third grade, my teacher Mr. R suggested that because I was good at telling stories, I could be a writer.

"A writer," I said with a laugh. "I can't even spell. Are you out of your goddamn mind?"

"Screw spelling" was his response.

But most of my teachers were not like Mr. R. They were not bad people; in fact, most were the opposite. Most were the best people who had decided to dedicate their lives to children. They were just doing what the textbook said to do, that's all. That medical model is still with us, and it defines disability as a property of the individual body that requires intervention and correction. I lost my sense of self to this perfect storm, because I knew from the start that no matter what my mom said, I wasn't *different* but *deficient*.

———

My experience of correction is just a short blip in a long history of invasive treatments designed to norm the round peg. In the normalizing society, as Sharon L. Snyder and David T. Mitchell wrote, differences of all kinds are turned into deficiencies and anomalies to be eradicated. Here are just a few examples. Treatments to cure the "abnormality" of homosexuality, from the nineteenth century to the *present day*, include hysterectomy, vasectomy, castration, clitoridectomy, chemical castration, blistering of the vulva, electric shock, nausea-inducing drugs, lobotomies, prayer, and conversion therapy.

In one example I read about, a boy named Michael liked to play with "girl" toys. This concerned his parents, so they took him to gender psychiatrists, where Michael was watched through one-way mirrors and his mother was told to ignore him if he wanted to play with gender nonconforming toys. At home, these experts organized a behavior modification program, which included Michael being spanked by his father if he engaged in gender nonconforming behavior.

Here is a description of a father's hearing treatment for his deaf daughter from 1990: "At the speech and hearing clinic I was trained to bind the mind of my daughter. Like the twisting of feet into lotus hooks, I was encouraged to force her deaf mind into a hearing shape. I must withhold recognition of her most eloquent gestures until she makes a sound, any sound. I must force her to wear hearing aids no matter how she struggles against them. The shape of a hearing mind is so much more attractive."

In the twentieth century, so-called abnormal brains were targeted for correction through lobotomies, a "surgery" that involves severing connections in the brain's prefrontal cortex. Beginning in the early 1950s, a doctor named Walter J. Freeman would travel from state to state performing lobotomies in people's homes. In one description of the surgery, Dr. Freeman asked a patient to tilt back her head. He proceeded to take out an ice pick, which he simply wiped off with a rag, then jammed the ice pick through her eye socket, into the lower regions of her frontal lobe. He jerked it around, removed it, wiped it with the rag, put his hat on, and was paid. From the fifties until the late sixties, Freeman performed 3,439 lobotomies in twenty-three states, despite the fact that he had no formal surgical training. Of these, 60 percent were performed on people with diagnoses of mental differences and 40 percent on people considered homosexual. There was a 14 percent fatality rate.

Even today, these attempts at correction continue: my friend Debbie has a daughter named Sue with Down syndrome. A social worker from the state of Ohio visited her after Sue was born and gave her a number of suggestions to "fix" her child, including counting her daily steps; physically restraining her; reminding her, as she grew up, that she had a genetic disorder; keeping expectations for school and work success low; and implementing a behavior modification system that included withholding affection, physical contact, and love.

On the surface, these stories of correction might seem different, but really, at their core, they are all the same. To be abnormal is to be delegitimized as a full human being, and to be made normal through remediation and intervention hurts. When a human being is pathologized, they become less than human, and then we humans do terrible things.

———

So when does the round peg, made to fit the square hole, finally break? Sometime in October 1988, during my sixth-grade year, I started to dissociate. I often felt as if I were in the corner of a room watching myself. I started to rub my eyebrow raw and became obsessed with my split ends and would pull out any irregular hairs. I thought I had cancer, and then AIDS, because I found some white spots on my tongue. Early that year, a teacher—whose name I cannot recall, thanks to that dissociation—assigned us the task of writing a story. I figured this was my chance to prove them all wrong. I wanted to show them that I was more than my speech problem, my chicken-scratch handwriting, and my fetus-level phonic awareness. I would show them I was a writer. And writers aren't stupid.

I went home that day, sat down, and tried to write all of the images, sounds, and feelings that were swirling around in my head. But it didn't work. Most of the words in my head never made it onto the page, and the ones that did were in the wrong place. So I did what I had always done: dumbed it down by using only the words I could find written around the room. I would write monosyllabic three-word sentences that even my terrible handwriting couldn't destroy. I would once more live up to the low expectations that had been set for me. I would again become the kind of kid they said I was. After an hour, my mom came into my room.

"What are you working on?" she asked.

"A story," I said.

Her eyes lit up, because she knew the stories I could tell. She, too, thought this was my chance. She looked at my paper. There was nothing on it.

"What's wrong?" she asked.

"I just can't write what's in my head," I said.

"Then don't write," she said. "Tell it to me."

I could do that?

"What the hell do you think humans used to do sitting around the fire to take their minds off getting eaten by a fucking saber-toothed tiger. Humans *told* stories. They did not write them down. There were no pencils. Of course you can do that!"

So I did. I dictated a ten-page story about King Arthur and the Knights of the Round Table to my mom. It was my magnum opus. A few weeks later, after I turned it in, the principal came into my classroom and whispered something to my teacher. Her eyes darted in my direction and she nodded. My teacher walked slowly back to my desk and said that the principal wanted to see me.

"Why?" I asked.

"To talk about your story," she said.

I jumped out of my chair, because I just knew I was being summoned to the principal because I had written the best story in the history of Pennekamp Elementary School. I was going to be given the Pennekamp Prose Award and have a plaque hung in my honor in the front of the school. That is how good my story was. I had crushed it. I swear to God, I gave the kid in the front row a high five on the way out the door.

When I got to the principal's office, my mom was there. She, too, it seemed, had been summoned to part take in my glory—*our* glory. We had proved them wrong, together, and this was their mea culpa. Better late than never. I sat down.

"Jonathan," the principal said, "please tell us why you copied this story from someone else." My mom looked sad. She couldn't manage even one f-bomb, that's how sad she was. It scared me. So we walked out of the principal's office and out of that school for good.

I went home that afternoon and made my plan and wrote my note. It wasn't the most thought-out plan, but it was mine. I got a glass of water and a bottle of aspirin. I sat there and didn't feel anything. I turned on the light and walked over to my bird Charlie's cage to say goodbye. I took him out of his cage and said I was sorry. He kissed my face and said, "Hi, Jon, hi, Jon, hi, Jon, hi, Jon, hi, Jon." I put down the bottle of pills. I couldn't do this to him. Or my mom. They loved me—the round peg—just as I was, and that, for a moment, was enough.

———

I want you to know that most of the other kids I knew in special education and beyond with brain and body difference were lost to their correction. People with brain and body differences have the lowest graduation rates, highest incarceration rates, and highest unemployment out of any minority group.

This is not an individual but a systemic problem. Bias against people with atypical bodies and minds is central to a culture of normalization. A report by the National Disability Rights Network and the government accounting offices reveal numerous cases of special education abuse:

A fifteen-year-old boy with autism in Michigan died while being physically restrained at school by four school employees who pinned him down for 60–70 minutes on his stomach, with his hands held behind his back and his shoulders and legs held down. He became nonresponsive after 45 minutes but the restraint continued and he eventually stopped breathing.

Children in California were physically placed in a "time-out" room and were not allowed to use the restroom, if needed. This forced students to sit in their own urine if they were unable to "hold" themselves.

In a rural school district in California, a ten-year-old non-verbal boy with multiple disabilities was tied to his wheelchair and left in the school van in the parking lot for hours on two separate days. His wrists were tied to the arms of his wheelchair with components removed from the safety vest used during transport on the van. His legs were bound together at the ankles with a nylon Velcro strap. On an unscheduled visit to the school, his mother was outraged when she found him unsupervised, alone, bound to his wheelchair in the van.

In California, a classroom aide dragged a nine-year-old child with Down syndrome across the play yard. The student sustained significant skin abrasions to his lower back and upper buttocks requiring medical care.

A behavior tech broke the arm of a boy who has bipolar disorder and autism while attempting to restrain him. The boy suffered a "spiral fracture to the upper right arm," according to emergency room staff. He was taken to his after-school program by a bus aide who told police he cried the entire ride.

Children in North Carolina with mental illness were being taped to chairs and locked in closets by teachers.

Forty-one percent of states have no laws or guidelines regarding restraint or seclusion in public school.

Ninety percent of states allow restraints.

And students with disabilities are physically punished at disproportionate rates to the general population.

It goes well beyond special education. A report by the Ruderman Family Foundation shows that half of police shootings have involved a person with a cognitive or physical difference. Women with intellectual disabilities are twenty-two times more likely to be victims of sexual violence or raped than the general population. "Diagnostic" terms from the great sorting of humans such as *retard, idiot,* and *moron* are commonly and cavalierly used in popular culture. And people with disabilities are substantially more likely than the general population to be unemployed and victims of abuse and hate crimes.

Evidence of a tragedy? No. A crime.

My mom, my dad, Steve, Elliot, and I and millions of others are caught in the cycle of a massive system of normalization. This system has, ironically (or not), become normal to us and penetrates the heart of our culture. We know more than ever about the long-term effects of systemic sexism and racism. But do we fully understand, and condemn, the effects of systemic ableism? Do we even call it that? I don't think so. In 2001, the United States Supreme Court ruled in *Board of Trustees of the University of Alabama v. Garrett* that there was no history of systemic discrimination against people with disabilities. This despite the fact that, beginning in the 1880s and lasting until the 1970s, hundreds of cities adopted so-called ugly laws that specifically banned many people with physical differences from public.

Here is Chicago's: "Any person who is diseased, maimed, mutilated, or in any way deformed so as to be an unsightly or disgusting object, or an improper person to be allowed in or on the streets, highways, thoroughfares, or public places in this city, shall not therein or thereon expose himself to public view, under the penalty of $1 for each offense."

As sociologist Bill Hughes wrote, the lives of those with brain and body differences have been blighted and demeaned by a degree of supervision that is without historical parallel: they've been pathologized by medicine and put in "special" spaces. No one is left un-normed as the system of normal churns. Normal is enforced through the subjugation of the abnormal, of course, but the disabled as a social category walls off human imperfection and "treats" it, affirming the illusion that all bodies and minds can and should be the same.

To be abnormal is to be told that you should be other than you are. To norm means to make regular. And we are continually doing this to anyone who does not meet the arbitrary standard of normal: made, through force, into something, or someone, you are not.

— IV —

Normed

They done me wrong. They done us all wrong.
> —Carrie Buck, inmate number 1692
> of the Virginia State Colony for
> Epileptics and Feebleminded

For it is quite conceivable ... that one fine day a highly organized and mechanized humanity will conclude quite democratically ... that for humanity as a whole it would be better to liquidate certain parts thereof.
> —Hannah Arendt,
> *The Origins of Totalitarianism*

In the fall of 2010, I gave a keynote address for the Williams Syndrome Association. Williams Syndrome (WS) is a genetic condition characterized by a number of medical problems, including cardiovascular disease, developmental delays, and learning challenges. These often occur side by side with striking verbal abilities, and, as I would soon learn, highly social and exuberant personalities.

Michele, a young woman with WS, and her father, Bill, met me at registration. "YOU ARE LIKE THE BEST WRITER EVER AND THE BEST SPEAKER EVER. WE LOVE YOU!" Michele screamed as she bear-hugged me. Bill shook my hand and said, "If you don't get a standing ovation here, you really, really suck!"

We grabbed lunch, and I learned about Michele's life with WS. She worked as a saleswoman at a small women's clothing store in her hometown ("IT IS LIKE THE BEST!"), lived with her parents ("I LOOOOOVE THEM SOOOOOO MUCH!"), and had a boyfriend ("WE WILL BE TOGETHER FOREVER"). Michelle had a life-threatening cardiovascular issue and struggled with cognitive tasks such as spatial relations, number manipulation, and abstract reasoning. She would most likely never live on her own. But Michele was happy. And so was Bill. According to the Williams Syndrome Association, more than 95 percent of parents of kids like Michele say that the joy and perspective a child with WS brings into their lives had been unimaginable.

After lunch, they escorted me to the keynote speaker reception. These usually suck big-time. Not this one. If you haven't been to a party with five hundred people with WS, you haven't lived. A gathering of people with WS is part rock concert (WS folks love music), part Burning Man, part rave, part Mickey Mouse fun house on ecstasy. It was hands down the best, most joyful party I had ever seen. When I had to leave, Michele gave me one last hug. Bill looked sad. I asked what was going on, and he shared a number of trends that deeply concerned the WS community. Mainstream medicine is extremely negative about WS; more than 95 percent of pregnancies "diagnosed" with WS are terminated, and WS has been identified by a number of genetic associations as a "curable" disorder through genetic engineering. Bill pointed to the crowd and said, "They just might be an endangered species."

Don't fool yourself—just because normal isn't fact doesn't mean it hasn't been *used* as fact. To correct difference is always to eliminate difference.

———

I have alluded to this darkness in individual cases of violent ways difference has been destroyed. Beginning in the early twentieth century, something darker and more systematic emerged: a movement to eliminate brain and body differences called eugenics. A catchy word, yes, which would make a great name for a preschool, were it not so evil.

While its scope was large, and its history complicated, the purpose of the eugenics movement was simple: rid the world of defectives. I know this may sound dramatic—because this movement is not as widely understood and condemned as it should be. The eugenics movement hasn't been fully included in the crimes committed against minority groups. But it is a crime, and we need to know its history, because it does not only exist in the past.

And here is where I say, brace yourself for stories that seem like outtakes from George Orwell's *1984* and clinically insidious words such as *defectives* and *feebleminded*. Most eugenicists could moonlight as dystopian novelists. Because of the strangeness rooted in the movement, eugenics has been hiding in plain sight for a long time.

The eugenics movement is linked to the great sorting of human traits in the nineteenth and twentieth centuries when statisticians were calculating norms and averages of humans, and shrinks and doctors were diagnosing and treating the people who ended up on the wrong side of the bell curve. During this time period, Darwin also revolutionized our understanding of where humans come from by arguing that evolution is driven by inherited traits that are selected, over long stretches of time, from "mutations" that prove to be advantageous to a specie's survival. This is a critical junction in the history of human differences, because Darwin himself was agnostic to the concept of mutation—it could be good or bad, depending on its outcome—and believed that human variation was *the* driver of evolution. Without some freaky, mutated zebra with a long neck to reach leaves on trees, we'd have no giraffes; without people who couldn't sit still, we'd have no California; and without some deviant apes with mutated brains that were bigger than the "normal" ape brain, we'd have no humans.

As we've seen, not everyone viewed variation, mutation, and difference as positive, or even as agnostic. Darwin's theory of evolution, driven by inherited traits, was taken up and contorted by the great sorters to argue that if traits are inherited, and if there are a whole bunch of people who suck because of their inherited traits, then those people have got to go. That was the argument of Herbert Spencer, the eugenics movement's founding intellectual. According to Wikipedia, Spencer was an "English philosopher, biologist, anthropologist, sociologist, and prominent political theorist of the Victorian age. What's left out is that Spencer was also a total dick. Spencer twisted Darwin's theory of evolution, named it "survival of the fittest," and ran with the idea, advocating for policies and laws that would achieve "Social Darwinism." In plain English, Spencer believed that "all imperfection must disappear."

The irony is, many of the most prominent eugenicists were extremely odd and strange, the very type of people targeted for elimination. We've seen this paradox before and will see it again. We'll see it right now, actually: Francis J. Galton, the man who created the term *eugenics*, is exhibit A of self-loathing. Galton, as I've already mentioned, was Darwin's cousin. He began his career as a doctor, then left medicine for the emerging field of statistics. The guy was super into counting. He actually had a motto that I'm considering turning into a T-shirt: "Whenever you can, count." And he did count, obsessively. He counted people fidgeting in the audience at his lectures, the number of waves in his bathtub, and ladies on the street with large chests ("I surveyed them in *every way* and tabulated the results at my leisure").

His obsession came at the right time in history. Statistics as a field of study was blowing up, and Galton jumped right in. He became an expert, with a focus on variability of human traits, and renamed Adolphe Quetelet's charts the "normal curve." Galton used the normal curve as a means of organizing observed patterns of heredity and identifying what he considered to be areas for improvement. He applied this passion for counting and inherited traits in a study of intelligence called "hereditary genius." He studied how traits such as intelligence and creativity were passed on within particular families. (Spoiler alert: he concluded that British white guys who like to count are smart.) He ended a letter with a rhetorical question that would eventually impact the entire world and turn out to be not so rhetorical after all: "Could not the undesirables be got rid of and the desirables multiplied?"

I hate rhetorical questions that are really statements. Give me a break, counting man; can't you just say what you think? Eventually Galton did come right out and began calling for the active improvement of the human race through the application of the emerging science of what we now call genetics. He called this eugenics, a combination of the Greek words for "well" and "born."

Galton did not go right into the heart of darkness that would become the eugenics movement. He was all about "positive eugenics"—an oxymoron if there ever was one—which were ways to optimize the right part of the bell curve by encouraging the wellborn to get it on! Galton proposed "strategic mating," "eugenic coupling," marriage laws to encourage "good breeding," and "social clubs" for wellborn people to meet and produce more of their kind.

I wish the story of eugenics ended here, with Galton counting boobs in a Victorian swingers club. Then we could all have a good laugh and call it a day. Sadly, that's not where the story ends, not even close. Galton's term caught on, and its logic was applied to the other end of the normal distribution curve. Forget the right people getting it on; let's do something about those imperfections.

How negative eugenics, as it came to be known, emerged as the focus of the movement is, on one hand, complicated, involving many different fields of science and points of view, all occurring within a context of massive social disruptions. But on the other hand, it's not complicated at all. We like having people exist lower on the pecking order than we do. And so the great sorting of humans into categories of deficiency gave eugenicists the perfect target: the abnormals and defectives.

Truth be told, Spencer and Galton were mostly just talk. Remember, they *were* British. And eugenics, as a movement, was mostly talk until it came to America. Americans are not talkers, however; we're doers. When it came to doing eugenics, we got it done. The man responsible for this was Charles Davenport. He did not invent American eugenics—it was already stewing in the hot mess of racism, anti-immigrant sentiment, and urbanization of early-twentieth-century America (as 18 million people arrived in the new country between 1890 and 1920)—but he led it.

So who was this man? Davenport was from the best genetic stock, as if Charles Darwin met Gregor Mendel, the strapping Augustinian friar and founder of modern genetics, and conceived Davenport in a eugenic sex club as Galton "counted" in the corner. He was an eminent biologist, chair of Harvard's biology department, and had published widely in the most respected scientific journals of the day.

Just kidding.

Davenport was a zoologist. He was the director of the Brooklyn Institute of Arts and Sciences Biological Laboratory in Cold Spring Harbor, Long Island, located more than an hour's train-and-buggy ride into the wilderness. The Harvard of Long Island it was not. Davenport's research consisted of studying the Australian marine pill bug, oysters, and winter flounder, which we all know are so similar to humans that he was definitely qualified to judge people, too.

In the course of his research, he came across Galton's theories and became a big fan, and he even tried to meet with him in London. But Davenport was constantly rejected by Galton due to his lack of scientific credentials and social class. Davenport was also openly racist, which went hand in hand with being a eugenicist. He believed the laws of generic inheritance could be used to make the unfit "disappear." His mantra was "We need more protoplasm." What protoplasm was, he really didn't say, and I still don't know what the hell that means. I think he just thought it made a better chant than, say, "We need more normal white people."

Davenport's big break came in 1902, the same year that Andrew Carnegie sold his steel company and created the Carnegie Institution, which was later renamed the Carnegie Institution of Washington. This was the largest philanthropic entity of its kind at the time, and it became one of the primary scientific research organizations in the world. Just months after the Carnegie Institution was founded, Davenport approached the organization to fund a "biological experiment station" at Cold Spring Harbor. On the face of it, Davenport's proposal was to study evolution, but the devil was hidden in the details. Okay, so he didn't actually hide it that well, writing, "the aim of this establishment would be the analytic and expiration study of . . . race change," and "improvements of the human race can probably be effected only by understanding and applying these methods."

Davenport received funding to create what became the Eugenics Records Office at Cold Spring Harbor. This is super ironic considering the fact that Andrew Carnegie, a Scottish immigrant who could hardly read when he came to America, would have been high on the eugenics defective list. Irony aside, the Eugenics Records Office (ERO), run by an unqualified man on a remote harbor on Long Island, became the center of the eugenics movement, which grew to include organizations like the American Eugenics Society. It was supported not only by the Carnegie Institution, but also by a who's who of American philanthropy, industry, academics, and government, including the Rockefeller Foundation, the Harriman family (the third richest family in the United States), Harvard, Princeton, Yale, Stanford, the American Medical Association, the American Genetic Association, and the United States Department of State.

Through the ERO, over many years, Davenport and others distilled the strands of genetic and eugenic theory into a simple, digestible message: defectives are destroying the world, genetic science has proven it doesn't have to be that way, so the defectives have *got* to go.

The office's stated purpose, according to investigative journalist Edwin Black, became "the registration of the genetic backgrounds of all Americans, separating the defective strains from the desired lineages." The Eugenics Records Office, however, was no mere research institute; it was the command center for a roundup. From there, Davenport led a national hunt for the "abnormal," the "feebleminded," the "unfit," and the "defective." Or what he called when he was in his Orwellian mood "the great strains for human protoplasm that are surging through the country." A team of field workers spread out across the country to find what they called the "submerged 10th" of the normal curve.

Who were these defectives? One eugenicist believed that "abnormal children are those afflicted with anything whatsoever that unfavorably affects their lives in relation to the social medium in which they live." Wow, that's broad. But super scientific. I mean they used big words, so it must be true. I get it. Who else? Stutterers, the poor, people for whom English was a second language, the nonverbal, people with migraines, people who have fainting spells, people with environmental-borne illnesses such as tuberculosis, anyone with congenital conditions such as a club foot, people who are deaf or blind or have reading problems, people with Down syndrome, epilepsy, depression, schizophrenia, alcoholism, immigrants, the unemployed, orphans, and children who underperform in the public school system.

To find the "defectives in our midst" (another catchy phrase that I think inspired the movie title *Gorillas in the Mist*), Davenport and other eugenicists built a national surveillance network by drawing on thousands of records from charity organizations, 42 institutions for the feebleminded, 115 schools for the deaf, 350 hospitals for the insane, 1,200 refugee homes, 1,300 prisons, 1,500 hospitals, 2,500 almshouses, and more than 1,000 schools to create more than one hundred Fitter Families Contests. What are these? Think state fair livestock competitions for people: competitors submitted an "Abridged Record of Family Traits," and a team of medical doctors performed psychological and physical exams on family members. Each family member was given an overall letter grade of eugenic health, and the family with the highest grade average was awarded a silver trophy. All contestants with a B+ or better received bronze medals bearing the inscription *Yeah,*

I have good heritage. If you didn't have a good heritage? You, Pa, and Ma got thrown into the wheat thrasher and fed to the blue-ribbon pig.

Kidding, not kidding.

If you failed the test, they did have a plan for you. It did not involve being fed to livestock, but it was real, called "The Best Practical Means for Cutting Off the Defective Germ-Plasms of the American Population." This masterpiece of dystopian literature had eighteen actions to cut off said germ plasm. Some of these were leftovers from the good old positive eugenic days, such as polygamy and strategic mating. But most were negative eugenics at its most draconian: ban "non-eugenic" marriages, then incarcerate, sterilize, and eliminate the defectives.

The marriage one, to be fair, was really low-hanging fruit for this group of social visionaries. The state of Connecticut in 1895 banned non-eugenic marriages, which were, as the journalist Adam Cohen wrote, punishable with three years in prison for the married and five years in prison for anyone who aided in such a marriage. By 1930, forty-one states had similar bans.

Next on the list: lock 'em up. Their words, not mine: "It is possible to colonize all of our feeble minded person under conditions in which they would be perfectly happy." Another guy described the incarceration part of the plan as "Permanent sequestration under happiest conditions," which sounds like an S and M club that gives out dystopian fortune cookies. By 1914, thirty-six states had institutions for the feebleminded and the remaining had some system in place to manage their sub-normal population. According to Sharon L. Snyder and David T. Mitchell, by 1923, 60 percent of the identified "feebleminded" population had been incarcerated, and by 1939, 74 percent had been locked up. As the sociologist James Trent documented in his book *Inventing the Feeble Mind*, at their peak in 1967, the large public institutions in the United States for the feebleminded held nearly 200,300 defectives, with the full support of local, state, and federal government.

To be fair to our friends the eugenicists, not all of them were fire-and-brimstone, double-speaking, incarcerating tyrants. Many had only the best interests of the "defectives" in mind. Martin Barr, for example, the head of one of the country's largest institutions, wanted only the best for the "abnormals." Permanent segregation didn't have to be bad. He believed the abnormal should have an island to call their own: "Might not a permanent colony be found—either on one of the newly acquired islands, the unoccupied lands of the Atlantic seaboard, or the far west which, under proper regulation, could be made a true haven of irresponsibility." These colonies would be a utopia where the defectives "in the possession of an assured freedom—always under careful direction and supervision—enjoy happiness."

Utopia, however, these institutions were not. One father described visiting his son in an institution in Massachusetts called Belchertown. He saw "naked patients smeared with urine, feces, and food, vomit-encrusted sheets" and "maggots wriggling inside or crawling out of the infected ears of several helpless, profoundly retarded persons while they lay in their crib-beds." A state official, Joseph Tauro, was assigned to investigate Belchertown, and, after he visited the school unannounced, corroborated the father's claims, adding that he saw "a little girl drinking from a feces-filled commode."

This was in 1971.

———

Though they talked a big game about their island colonies, the eugenics movement was always really about *eliminating* abnormals. Don't take my word for it; take theirs, as written in the publication I mentioned earlier: *The Best Practical Means for Cutting Off the Defective Germ-Plasms of the American Population.*

This plan outlined eighteen actions to "eliminate" defective germplasm. Segregation and institutionalization were generally the top means for elimination; the head of a North Carolina school for the feebleminded said as much: "The ultimate aim of the school is the *elimination* of feeblemindedness from the race by segregation." That was actually the tag line for his annual report. He and others did a bang-up job. These institutions were called by one reporter "euthanasia through neglect." At one institution in Illinois, within two months of admittance, 10 percent of those institutionalized died, with some places having up to a 40 percent mortality rate. In the 1990s, according to Edwin Black's research, the average life expectancy for those who would have been considered feebleminded was 66.2 years. During the mid-twentieth century, at the height of the eugenics movement, it was 18.5 years.

Elimination through segregation, though effective, was slow and costly. So, in January 1914, the eugenics movement rolled out a new, bolder idea: prevent the defectives from even being born. They chose the first-ever national conference on race betterment to make the big announcement. This was the largest eugenics conference ever held in the United States and involved four hundred delegates and thousands of members of the general public. People had to be turned away. It was fun for the whole normal family. Activities included mental and physical perfection contests, in which babies were given IQ tests. It was here that a guy named Harry Laughlin, number two at the Eugenic Records Office—who, by the way, was an epileptic, one of the differences most targeted by eugenics for elimination—presented the future of the movement by sharing "calculations on the working out of a proposed program of sterilization."

Awkward eugenic speak aside, this was as clear as clear can be: the eugenics movement would now turn its attention to sterilizing the abnormal. This plan wasn't the first time sterilization had been proposed for defectives. In 1894, a Kansas physician named Dr. Hoyt Pilcher was the first in modern times to use castration as a way to prevent procreation, which gives a whole other meaning to "what's the matter with Kansas." He was superintendent of the Kansas State Home for the Feebleminded when he castrated fifty-eight *children*. This was completely against the law, but his supervisors defended him, saying, "Those who are now criticizing Dr. Pilcher will in a few years be talking of erecting a monument to his memory." *Erecting* was a poor choice of words. The National Association of Institutions for the Feeble-Minded praised him as "courageous."

Laughlin's plan, however, was much more serious and systemic than just one sadistic doctor with a butcher knife in Topeka. This plan included a model sterilization law designed to be a constitutionally sound template for any state committed to a sterilization program. The law targeted for sterilization not only the "defective" but also the "socially inadequate," defined as anyone "regardless of etiology or prognosis who fails chronically in comparison with normal persons to maintain himself or herself as a useful member of the organized social life of the state." The plan also included an outreach strategy to a broad range of institutions that could find the unfit. Leaders of the optometry profession made a plan to register, round up, and coercively sterilize every relative of every American with hereditary blindness and other visual impairments. Pediatricians joined the movement by conducting screenings and IQ tests on infants. A school-to-operating-table pipeline was developed, through extensive partnerships with more than one thousand public schools throughout the country committed to identifying struggling students and other "defectives" and referring them to specialized institutions for the "feebleminded."

In total, more than 15 million people were identified as candidates for sterilization.

The plan was a big hit and was memorialized in a popular eugenics poem:

> *Oh, you wise men, take up the burden*
> *And make this your loudest creed,*
> *Sterilize the misfits promptly—*
> *All not fit to breed.*

The first sterilization law was passed in Indiana in 1907, and similar laws eventually passed in thirty-two other states. Some three thousand *involuntary* sterilization procedures were performed from 1925 to 1927 alone, often with total disregard for the "patient's" well-being. A man named Buck Smith who was sterilized in Virginia said: "They gave me some pills that made me drowsy and then they wheeled me up to the operating table. The doctor said, 'Buck, I'm going to have to tie your tubes and then maybe you'll be able to go home.'" Buck witnessed the procedure. The doctor pinched his scrotum and made a small incision. "I watched the whole thing. I was awake the whole time." Surely this was illegal, right? The eugenics movement was prepared for that charge and had a plan to test, and hopefully prove, the constitutionality of coerced sterilization. They believed that if the Supreme Court ruled sterilization was legal, then the practice would spread throughout the country.

The movement got its chance in 1927 with the sterilization of a woman named Carrie Buck, inmate 1692 of the Colony for the Epileptic and Feebleminded near Lynchburg,

Virginia, the nation's largest facility of its kind and the state's greatest center of sterilization. Carrie found herself in the colony for the same reasons others did—she was poor, she was considered "uneducated," and, because she had a daughter without being married, she was considered "morally defective." Her mother, Emma, was also an inmate at the colony. This family history was a eugenicist's dream, because they believed it proved that Carrie's defects were inherited and thus could be prevented through sterilization from spreading. To the eugenicists' great joy, not only was Carrie "defective," but so, they believed, was her daughter, Vivian. Carrie Buck was the perfect pawn for the eugenics game of Supreme Court chess.

On October 19, 1927, Carrie was sterilized, in a procedure that followed to the letter the model sterilization law developed by Laughlin. Then the former legal counsel for the colony took the colony to court on *Carrie's* behalf. The stage was set for the eugenics movement to get their ruling that the sterilization of defectives was constitutional. The legality of Carrie Buck's sterilization came down to the assessment of her three-month-old daughter by a social worker. Here is the court transcript:

Judge: Have you an impression about the child?

Social worker: It is difficult to judge probabilities of a child as young as her but it seems to be not quite a normal baby.

Judge: You would not judge the child as a normal baby?

Social worker: There is a look about it that is not quite normal, but just what it is I can't tell.

That was all it took. Vivian was deemed defective like her mother and grandmother. Carrie's case was eventually taken to the US Supreme Court and is known as *Buck vs. Bell*. In the spring of 1927, the court ruled that Carrie Buck's sterilization was constitutional. The majority opinion was written by Oliver Wendell Holmes, who argued that the state had a right to involuntarily sterilize American citizens. The following paragraph from Holmes's opinion might as well have been the forward to a eugenic manifesto: "It is better for all the world, if instead of waiting to execute degenerate off-spring for crime, or to let them starve for their imbecility, society can prevent those who are manifestly unfit from continuing their kind. Three generations of imbeciles are enough." The rate of sterilization exploded after the Supreme Court ruling. Almost seventy thousand people were sterilized. In case you were interested, Vivian went on to become an honors student.

———

The United States Supreme Court ruled that the state had the right to eliminate forms of difference through sterilization. Isn't that the bottom of the well? Unfortunately, it's not. The stated purpose of the eugenics movement from the beginning was the elimination of the abnormal. They never hid this fact: "It would be an act of kindness and a protection to the state if [defectives] could be killed." This is from their official journal, *Institution Quarterly*.

So why not kill them? Well, that, too, was in the plan. Point eight of *The Best Practical Means for Cutting Off the Defective Germ-plasms of the American Population* was euthanasia or "painless killing" of people deemed worthless. I hate to be a nag, but this is not euthanasia, a term that typically means ending the life of someone or something with a terminal condition. This is murder.

Killing defectives eventually went the way you knew it would: Hollywood. Yep, in 1917, the movement got its own movie called *The Black Stork*. This film is about a eugenically mismatched couple who are told not to have children because they are likely to be defective. The couple ignores this warning, gives birth to a "defective child," and then lets it die. The movie is based on the life and work of Harry J. Haiselden, the chief surgeon at the German-American Hospital in Chicago, who killed infants for "eugenic" reasons. Haiselden left newborn infants' umbilical cords untied so they could bleed to death and injected other infants with opiates. When traveling on a eugenic lecture tour, the doctor sent instructions to his staff, via cross-country telegraphs, on which babies to kill, without seeing the patients. He played himself in *The Black Stork*. The movie was screened all day in Chicago from 9:00 a.m. to 10:00 p.m. when it premiered, and played in theaters around the country for more than a decade. Its tagline: "Kill defectives, save the nation, and see *The Black Stork*."

The eugenics movement gave voice, form, logic, and respectability to a historic dehumanization of people with differences. However, much to the dismay of eugenicists, the blatant killing of defectives never really took off in America. But it did elsewhere. Who was a huge fan? Drumroll, please: Adolf Hitler. Yeah. That Hitler. He called a popular eugenics book "his bible" and wrote the author a fan letter. Davenport and others were in constant contact with German race hygienists, and a 1934 letter from C. M. Goethe to a colleague celebrated eugenics thought leaders for inspiring Nazi Germany: "You will be interested to know that your work has played a powerful part in shaping the opinions of the group of intellectuals who are behind Hitler in this epoch-making program. Everywhere I sensed that opinions have been tremendously stimulated by American thought and particularly by the work of the Human Betterment Foundation. I want you, my dear friend, to carry this thought with you for the rest of your life, that you have really jolted into action a great government."

For the rest of their life, indeed.

As the historian Edith Sheffer wrote, the Third Reich was a diagnosis regime: "The state became obsessed with sorting the population into categories, cataloguing people by race, politics, religion, sexuality, criminality, heredity, and biologic defects. These labels, then, become the basis of individual persecution and extermination."

On July 14, 1933, Germany issued a mass compulsory sterilization statute, Part 1, No. 86, the Law for the Prevention of

Defective Progeny. Four hundred thousand Germans would be immediately subjected to the procedure, which became known as Hitler's cut. In 1934, the Third Reich sterilized at least fifty-six thousand people, one out of every twelve hundred Germans. By the end of the war, three hundred seventy-five thousand Germans had been sterilized. This was, according to the Third Reich, an "American-model sterilization law."

On August 18, 1939, the Reich ministry of the interior issued a decree that mandated all German doctors, nurses, health officials, and midwives report any so-called *Ausschuss-kinderer*, or "garbage children," who had been born with certain supposedly hereditary disabilities such as "mental retardation," "physical deformity," "idiocy," and "malformations of all kinds." After being reported, the children entered one of the thirty-seven "special children's wards" for observation, where a panel of "medical experts" decided which of those children should live or die. These experts were paid for each child reported and often received a bonus for each child killed.

A survivor's drawing from the 1970s—a first-person historical document of the child killings—shows a group of children huddled in a corner. One holds a teddy bear. Another sucks his thumb. Next to them is a table where doctors are reading files and deciding who should die. Next to the table is a pile of clothes and items, including a stuffed animal, from children who have gone before. Next to the pile of clothes is a child being taken out of the room screaming.

The children selected for death were sent to pediatric killing wards where they were murdered by lethal injection or placed in hunger houses, where they died from malnutrition and starvation. They were also tortured and experimented on. As Suzanne Evans wrote, "Sometimes the children's blood and spinal fluids were drawn while they were still alive and replaced with air so that clear X-rays could be taken of their brains." Almost twenty-five thousand children were murdered.

In October 1939, Hitler signed the order for the T4 Program. This program specifically targeted for extermination adults considered abnormal and disabled, including those diagnosed with such conditions as epilepsy, physical malformation, insanity, feeblemindedness, depression, and alcoholism. There were six primary killing centers across Germany: Brandenburg, Grageneck, Hadamar, Bernburg, Sonnensiten, and Hartheim Castle. As Sharon L. Snyder and David T. Mitchell describe, based on original archival research, "there was an elaborate technology of murder that included a processing procedure that falsified death records; a gas chamber for the 'efficient' execution of many individuals at one time; an autopsy room for the advancement of medical 'knowledge' and the lucrative extraction of gold teeth; a body stacking room; and, finally, crematoria ovens." These are the same technologies and procedures that would be used for Hitler's "final solution."

The killing program for the abnormal was officially "halted" on August 24, 1941, but the Nazi regime continued killing people with differences in other regions and by other means. During what is called the "wild euthanasia period," patients with disabilities in Germany and the occupied territories were "shot, burned, frozen, starved, tortured, or poisoned to death."

In all, more than 750,000 "abnormal" or "defective" individuals were murdered. This has never been condemned as a crime against humanity. After the war, as Suzanne Evans documented, disabled victims were not recognized by government or legal authorities as persons who had been persecuted by the Nazi regime and received no restitution. There is no dedicated memorial of these crimes. None of the doctors who participated in the killing outside of concentration camps were prosecuted.

—

Am I wrong to pull this dark thread of the past into the present and argue that the violence of the norm is woven deeply into the fabric of who we are today?

You tell me.

According to historian Edith Sheffer, "doctors who worked during the Nazi era named at least thirty eponymous neurological and psychiatric diagnoses that are still used and diagnosed today."

In the mid-1990s, renowned moral philosophers Peter Singer and Jeffrie Murphy questioned the humanity of people with disabilities. Singer has referred to a disabled child as "it," arguing that the killing of a disabled child is "quite reasonable." Murphy wrote an article titled "Do the Retarded Have a Right to be Eaten?"

More than 30 percent of individuals in prison and 40 percent of those in jail have a cognitive or physical difference or mental illness.

Most of the 376 eugenics departments at American universities and professional associations have become genetics departments and organizations.

Oregon ordered its last forced sterilization in 1981 and had a Board of Eugenics until 1983. California continued to sterilize state prisoners between 2006 and 2010.

Buck vs. Bell has never been overruled or limited. According to Cohen, "federal courts are still ruling that the government has the right to forcibly sterilize, citing *Buck vs. Bell*" as precedent.

James Watson, the father of modern genetics and a Nobel laureate, studied at Cold Spring Harbor, the former home of the Eugenics Records Office, and became director in 1968. In 2003, he told a film crew that "if you are really stupid, I would call that a disease. So I'd like to get rid of that to help the lower 10 percent." He also said, "People say it would be terrible if we made all girls pretty. I think it would be great."

Homosexuality was listed as a psychiatric disorder in the *Diagnostic and Statistical Manual* (DSM) until 1973.

Brain differences that genetic researchers and members of the media have described as possibly "curable" through genetic interventions currently or in the near future include dyslexia, Down syndrome, ADHD, learning disabilities, intellectual disabilities, Williams Syndrome, and many other conditions.

In 1994, the *American Journal of Human Genetics* warned, "there is a significant risk that there will be an increased sentiment of instituting eugenic measures in the United States."

Crisper, which sounds like the name for a rad new salad spinner but is in fact a gene editing technique, has been marketed, in part, as a tool to eliminate genes associated with a range of brain and body differences.

Up to 85 percent of fetuses diagnosed with Down syndrome are aborted.

———

For almost twenty years, stories of self-elimination have been told to me, emailed to me, messaged to me, and handed to me almost every week: a wrist cut for over an hour with a butter knife; a noose made out of Spider-Man sheets; a pellet gun put in the eye socket so there would be less blood; instructions to feed the goldfish, to walk the dog, to say goodbye to the janitor because he was the only person who said hello in the morning, to sleep with their stuffed animal so they wouldn't be lonely. And of course, I'm sorry. I love you. It hurts too much. These stories continue, unabated, relentlessly, because the values and beliefs about which humans are normal, and which are not, which gave us the horrors of the eugenics movement are still with us today.

— V —

Act Normal

To the degree that the individual maintains a show before others that he himself does not believe, he can come to experience a special kind of alienation from self and a special kind of wariness of others.

—Erving Goffman,
*The Presentation of Self
in Everyday Life*

Normality is a paved road: It's comfortable to walk, but no flowers grow on it.

—Vincent van Gogh

Not long ago, you asked about my dad. You asked who he was. I couldn't answer you then. But I am ready to now. My dad is the kind of man who carried a very old-school briefcase. This briefcase felt smart. It even smelled smart, like worn leather from a chair in an Ivy League library. It was square, like a lock box, with a brass clip and a combination lock with roman numerals.

But inside this case was a shit show of crazy that he hid from the world. In there you'd find remains of food that he carried with him at all times, because he claimed he was diabetic and had to monitor his blood sugar: hard-boiled eggs, egg shells, wilted heads of broccoli that he ate raw, empty cans of lentil soup, can openers, brown banana peels. There was weed and its paraphernalia—ash, buds, burnt pipes, a rusted screen covered in residue. There were the things he was hiding from my mom: notices from the IRS, overdue phone bills, Department of Water and Power notices to shut the water off, letters from strangers. And in the midst of all this were legal briefs, motions, contracts, and pages from law books, covered in lentil soup and smelling of weed. That was my dad.

My dad was the kind of dad who took me to his drug dealer's house, where there were big buckets of popcorn and a cap gun that the dealer fired like he was Scarface. These are not unhappy memories, because when stoned, my dad was for a brief moment his best self. For fleeting moments frozen in my memory, with his square, Irish Kennedy jaw, my dad was funny, charming, and nice. He was a person I wanted to be with, the person I wanted to be. But when it came to drugs and alcohol, some was never enough for my dad, and he used drugs because they worked. They made it hurt less. Until they didn't.

My dad is the kind of dad who cried a lot. At sports games. Reading a book. But mostly while watching movies. *Trading Places. Hoosiers. Lethal Weapon.* Anything with a dog. Anything he watched on an airplane. Anything with a dog, shown on an airplane, where the dog dies. Anything showing men showing emotion.

We watched a lot of movies together, and on Fridays, he sat in his rocking chair and drank Heinekens and I ate microwave popcorn. One of our favorite movies was *Victory*, staring Pelé, the Brazilian soccer star. The movie is about a group of multinational prisoners of war during WWII who challenge their SS guards to a soccer game as a distraction as they attempt to escape. Not only do they escape, but they also win the game with seconds left, with a bicycle kick by Pelé. It was based on a true story, and my dad and I loved that movie. It ends with a chant of "Victoire!"—French for victory—and I can still see my dad making the V with his hands, silently mouthing "Victoire!" with tears streaming down his face.

One night, by the end of the movie, I counted twenty empty green glass Heineken bottles next to his La-Z-Boy chair. In the kitchen, there was an empty liter of Jack Daniel's. In the middle of the night, I got up to go to the bathroom and found him on the floor covered in vomit, not breathing. I don't remember what happened after that. My dad is the kind of dad who tried to eliminate himself. My dad's story is all too common, because when we don't fit in, many of us believe we shouldn't exist, and we try, as my dad did, as I did, to disappear.

———

Some people believe that there is no way to untangle the knot of normal, to resist normal, because normal is a power that seizes life before it is lived, shapes the terms of the game before it is played, and makes our choices before we choose. Some of my heroes, people like Michel Foucault, people who gave me a language to extricate myself from normal's grip, come close to this nihilism, arguing that resistance to any form of power is just a form of capitulation. I've come close to this pessimism at times in my life, but I also found it a dead-end way to live. I don't have a fancy argument of why they are wrong, nor am I armed with big words, a PhD, a cool name, or a French accent.

What I do know is that there was a way out for me. I know that I don't feel stupid anymore. I don't believe I'm defective anymore. I don't hurt the way I hurt that day in my room with that bottle of pills anymore. There was for me, and there is for you, a way to, as the philosopher Judith Butler wrote, "work the trap that one is inevitably in."

Normal must be resisted if you are ever going to live *your* life, as who you are, fully, in all your complexity.

———

Don't get me wrong, normal is a force of repression, for sure, but it is also a source of creation. One of the most common things said to children, especially children like me, is the mandate to "act normal," which is usually followed by a long list of things to *do* in order to play the role of a normal person: sit still, talk softer, raise your hand, wear the right clothes, play with the right toys, like the right colors. It's a never-ending set of commands that you can follow into the promised land of normality. I wonder if we recognize the irony of telling people to *act* normal, because to act is to perform a role that isn't real. And I wonder if we truly understand what it does to a human being to tell them to pretend to be someone, or something, they are not, and how this demand requires people to repress, efface, and cover up who they really are.

Resisting normal starts with a refusal to hide, to cover, to deny the parts of yourself that don't fit normal's story for you. Humans are made of jagged pieces that don't fit neatly together, and the challenge of anyone's life is to use all these pieces to make the biggest self one can. But there is a relentless pressure to solve the puzzle quickly, with as few pieces as possible. And so the most jagged, imperfect pieces get shoved under the rug. This hiding, however, doesn't work. Each jagged edge denied, each part taken as the whole, each big self narrowed, each multitude simplified, each circle squared is a small death and a sacrifice at the altar of normality that works for a while—until it doesn't. Because passing as normal never does.

Forcing human beings to perform normalcy, and then demanding that they self-police their normality, is part of normal's master plan. It's a form of social control achieved through self-surveillance for weight, height, reading rates, attention span, and sexuality, the averages for which are constantly fluctuating as we change ourselves to be in line. Again, normal is a moving target, and we are redrawing the lines for ourselves and everyone else all of the time. By acting normal, we pass for normal and become subjects willingly subjugated.

———

I know the cost of this self-policing, and passing, because I hid, not as an act of resistance, but as a tool of survival. I did not go back to school for a while after leaving Pennekamp Elementary. I went to another school for a minute and then stopped. I wasn't homeschooled but unschooled. I spent my days with my mom at her nonprofit organization called the South Bay Center for Counseling. My mom knew intuitively what John Holt, a former professor of education at Harvard, knew intellectually: for every day that school is toxic, it takes one day to heal. My mom knew something about healing because she was wounded, too.

My mom had what is fair to describe as a breakdown before I was born. She had just met my dad and moved with him to Bethesda, Maryland, so he could go to law school at Georgetown. There was an ugly custody battle between my mom and her ex-husband, and my mom was already riddled with Catholic guilt for getting a divorce in the first place.

My brother Billy roamed the streets with a pack of kids like a wild thing. My sister Kelly spent most of the day in the basement with her bunny named Midnight, and I'm not sure what my sister Michele did. One day my mom went into the bathtub and didn't come out. My sister Kelly brought her food and water and, some nights, slept on the floor next to the tub, holding my mom's hand. My mom's skin wilted like wet paper.

I don't know what helped her get out of that bathtub. My mom is a hard woman, of few words (unless you are a dog, in which case she will talk with you for hours in a high-pitched baby voice). My mother probably would have stayed—and died—in that bathroom if she hadn't found herself and her agency as a human being in helping others. After my father graduated from law school, the family moved back to San Francisco and my mom threw herself into radical social-justice politics. When we moved to Los Angeles, my mom volunteered at a hippie-dippie community mental health clinic above a psychic's shop, where people solved their own problems together. My mom loved that place and worked her way from volunteer to executive director, which she has been for the past forty years.

It was that place I went to when I left school. I had a lot of bad days, but my days at work with my mom were good. I watched movies in empty therapy rooms. I became friends with a therapist named Jim who had three fingers on his right hand and swore to me he blew the other two off throwing an M-80 firecracker at his school. I played soccer. I became a "teacher" at the center's therapeutic preschool for children who had experienced extreme trauma, and I was good at it. I had found, for a brief moment, a place to heal.

I knew, though, that this wouldn't last. I would have to go back to school. *It* started up again—what I now know is clinical anxiety. I rolled my eyes up into the back of my head; I rubbed my eyebrow raw; I convinced myself that Operation Desert Storm would lead to a nuclear holocaust; I kicked my soccer ball exactly one thousand times with both feet between 3:58 and 5:15 p.m. every day because if I didn't, someone I loved could die. I could not live the rest of my life at the center, so I made a plan to survive. I would go to a new school. I would not tell anyone about my differences. I would be normal.

In the fall of that year, I went to Hermosa Valley, a K–8 school. I did not tell anyone about what made me different, nor did my parents. I did not enroll in any special education services. My passing, of course, is part of a long history of people with difference being forced to hide these differences because of a social environment's hostility. Hiding our differences was a family tradition. My father tried to perform normalcy (terribly), my mother was in denial about her reading and writing challenges, and my siblings struggled with unnamed differences, set adrift to chase the horizon of the American dream.

Hiding, however, always comes at a cost. I lived in fear

because I could be caught any day through the smallest and most seemingly benign actions. For example, less than a month into my time at the new middle school, I learned that a girl named Johanna liked me. I know this will make me sound super old, but back then the thing to do when someone liked you was to send her a handwritten note with actual words, which was terrifying to me. So I came up with a plan to keep my note simple, to the point, and monosyllabic. I'd ask her how she was doing—but, as I said earlier, I did and still do have a bit of a problem with *how* versus *who*. So I wrote this note out four times. I read it to myself multiple times and passed it down the line of desks to Johanna. She unfolded it, read it, read it again, and crumpled it up. She laughed, and one of her friends turned to her and said, "He must be special." Note to self: use the phone next time.

———

When you hide, not only do you live in fear, but also in shame. You hide because of shame and then feel more shame and hide some more. Shame is a complicated emotion that has been working for the judges of normality and the self-police for a long time. For me, shame was repressive, driving me to conceal parts of myself, to tell myself to sit still, or talk quieter, or never write anything to anyone. My shame was also productive and led me to both hide my real self, and also create a false self. A writer I admire named Eve Sedgwick wrote, "One is *something* in experiencing shame." But, as Tobin Siebers wrote, being *something* is very different from being *someone*.

From middle school on, I was in search of *something* to be. The good news was that I had a something that helped me become a something, and that something was soccer. I had always been good at sports, but I was great at soccer. At first, the game was pure joy. I was a different person on the field, my weaknesses irrelevant and my strengths—which were ignored in school—actualized, named, and celebrated. I would not have survived if it wasn't for this game, but I almost didn't survive because of this game.

The feeling of recognition, of being seen, of success, was a drug for me. My mom felt this high, too, and sought out hit after hit. I don't judge her. Soccer was the way for her to show them all what she knew and they didn't: that I was good and valuable, that we were not just poor white trash. Intoxicated by this something, the rest of me went by the wayside, in pursuit of more. Eventually, though, when I didn't play well, my mom wouldn't speak to me for days.

Come high school, I was something that I don't even recognize now. When I was fourteen, we moved in the middle of my freshman year to Colorado. In a new place, I cobbled together a persona. I took to wearing Ralph Lauren polo shirts, various bro-like white hats, a braided leather belt (which was cool in 1993), white jean shorts (also cool), and sambas (always cool). I dated a blond, blue-eyed cheerleader from a respectable middle-class household and loved/hated her for it. I told no one about my differences. I did whatever I had to do to get through school, including spending ten hours on something that took most students one. I acted as if I did not care about learning, and I cheated. I put down others with differences—calling kids in special education retards, theater kids fags, using every misogynistic word there was. I'm sure I would have uttered racial slurs if there had been any students of color in the entire school. And, of course, I played soccer, all the time and at the expense of everything else. How did this work out?

At fifteen, I had an ulcer. I couldn't sleep. I lived either dissociated from my body or seized by it. A relentless voice in my head told me I was a stupid, crazy, lazy, fake, and a fraud. Come sixteen, I found drinking quieted these voices at first and then turned them louder. I made drinking a regular part of my life and kept it in check only because of the physical requirements of playing soccer. I am lucky for that. By my senior year, even soccer was falling apart. I played mediocre— for me—and the big Division 1 colleges that I thought would call didn't. My parents sent me to a therapist—a *sports* psychologist—to improve my game.

This something I became, that I don't recognize now, was not all of me, even then, of course. I loved horses. We had three and I took care of them. I was a peer counselor, encouraged to apply for the position by a man named Mr. T, who told me how he ate too fast because he couldn't stand dinnertime with his alcoholic father. I knew what he meant because I eat too fast, as well. I worked with a kid in middle school in special education who cut himself. My best friend, Jake, and I would sit in his basement and listen to U2 and Counting Crows (it was the nineties) and sing along. Somehow, somewhere, I got ahold of the Talking Heads' *Fear of Music*, and it lived in my yellow Walkman even as I told people I was listening to Hootie and the Blowfish. And, still, somewhere, buried under the something, was someone who loved to write and think. I ditched class and read (slowly) *East of Eden* in the bathroom. I wrote terrible poetry and plays at night when I couldn't sleep. But these pieces did not fit the something that I had become: by my senior year, my plan was to play soccer in college and become a high school soccer coach.

I'm lucky, though, that I had someone in my life who saw more of me, more *to* me, than I did. His name was Mr. P—later I'd call him Tim—and he was the AP English teacher at Green Mountain High School. He was the kind of old-school teacher that is an endangered species. He had a huge beard, wore Birkenstocks with socks, and named all of his own children after obscure J. D. Salinger characters. Mr. P was my senior year English teacher and was married to my junior year honors English teacher, Mrs. P. That woman hated me. My sophomore year I had applied to her class and was rejected. The application consisted of three handwritten and timed essays. When I didn't get in, my mom marched into the school. I sat outside of Mrs. P's office. I heard glass shattering. My mom walked out of the office and I was now in honors English.

The next year, Mrs. P made my life hell. In her class, spelling *did* count.

Toward the end of my year with Mrs. P, Tim asked to see me. I was sure it was to tell me that AP English, the next class after honors, wasn't for me. I walked in and took a seat. The Grateful Dead was playing in the background. "You should apply for AP English," Mr. P said. I laughed out loud. "You're joking, right? You've talked to your wife, right?" Mr. P stared at me for an uncomfortably long time without speaking. "I know how hard it is for you," he eventually said. "I know how hard you've had to work." I was filled with rage. "What the hell do you know about it?" I said. He looked me in the eye and said, "It's hard for me, too. Just like you." He knew. I had been found out. "I've seen your writing. You can't spell. But who cares? As Mark Twain said, never trust a man that can spell a word only one way."

I took AP English my senior year. Tim was the first person I told about my learning differences at that school, and he was the first person who accepted and accommodated these differences. Tim's class was an education in becoming the biggest self I could be. He had me read more than I thought I could, write, through dictation, more than I ever did before, and exposed me to more ways to be human than I ever knew existed. I had reclaimed, from the cutting-room floor, a thread to myself that I had abandoned. With his help, I began the long process of stitching myself back together into someone new.

Mr. P may have seen and recognized my multitudes and my value, but I hadn't fully. My challenge after high school was to tell a new story about myself, to myself, with the words of resistance that had been whispered in my ear by people who believed in me. It is hard to know who you are when the very core of yourself, your body and mind, have been disqualified as abnormal. And it is hard to shift through the social roles we are forced to play by the directors of the normal show.

After high school, I was stuck in this in-between, knowing what I was not, but not yet knowing what I could become. I graduated from Green Mountain High School in 1995, and I went to Loyola Marymount University (LMU) in Los Angeles. I went there to play soccer. I got *in* there to play soccer. Was this the real me? It was, in part, and I still loved to play, but I also knew that it was not all of me. I was a hot mess of shame, confusion, and self-destruction. The summer before college, while I was still living in Colorado, I was arrested for public intoxication and spent a night in a county jail. I don't remember how many nights I drove my truck the forty-five-minute route home from some party—on U.S. 85, the most dangerous federal highway in America—to wake up the next morning not knowing how I got home or how I was still alive.

The first day of soccer training camp, I severely sprained my ankle. I played the rest of the year hurt. My drinking continued. I knew soccer was not all that I was or wanted to be. But I was terrified of what would be left when that was taken away, because what was left was an anger that would consume me.

College was no better at first. My plan, as it had been in high school, was to overcome my differences through sheer force of will. Even today, I'm asked how I overcame my dyslexia. When I point out that to say I "overcame" dyslexia implies dyslexia is a bad thing, people just nod, not getting my point at all, agreeing that yes, it is a bad thing that needs to be overcome, and could I please tell them how I did so?

It is a deeply entrenched cultural narrative that differences need to be overcome. Literature and film are filled with characters with atypical minds and bodies who, when not used as tropes for pity, overcome their personal limitations through heroic effort. Popular images of athletes with disabilities perpetuate the myth of the "super cripple," and charity organizations raise money to help individuals overcome, or worse, cure their disabilities.

The "overcoming" story line has so many negative consequences. It puts the onus of change on the person, not the environment around the person. Those held up as "overcoming" their differences, usually at great personal cost, feed and affirm the myth that disability is something to overcome, shaming the vast majority of people who can't. I tried my first semester in college to overcome my problems. I stayed up most nights until one in the morning, sat in the front row, made myself sit still, took notes I couldn't read later. I read and reread papers that still were filled with misspelled words, and I almost failed out.

My mom had kept her job when we moved from Los Angeles to Colorado and commuted monthly. I don't know who my mom would be without her work. Whatever my mom's wound was, it never fully healed. I would hear it behind her words and see it behind her eyes when her defenses were down, which they never were for long. I've only seen my mom cry once. This was back in Colorado. I had come home from high school, it was snowing, and R.E.M.'s "Nightswimming" was playing in the background. She was so embarrassed, it was like I had seen her naked.

It's wrong to dismiss my mom's passion for her work as some sort of coping mechanism. Love and work were all that mattered, and in her work she had both. Maybe it was because of this that she asked me to work in one of the afterschool programs her organization ran in Los Angeles my first year in college. Maybe she knew that I wasn't overcoming anything but was succumbing to my own malignancy, much like hers. I took the job because I needed beer money.

The job was to work with at-risk children, many in special education, in an after-school program. I brought all of my baggage to that first job, to a bunch of kids sitting in a cafeteria in a school surrounded by barbed wire, with no books and tagged bathrooms. There were classrooms in converted storage closets and inspirational posters from the 1980s: "Life is 1% inspiration and 99% perspiration." "Just show up." "DARE." "Reading Is Fundamental."

For that first day, I had prepared all these academic interventions. I thought that if I had the right pedagogy—if everyone was just hooked on phonics—all would be better. I walked in and was faced with a handful of ten- to twelve-year-olds. I got up in front of the class, took my best *Stand and Deliver* pose, and jumped into some half-baked phonics lesson. I was in the zone. Diagramming sentences. Conjugating like Strunk and White. Going *chaa* and *ahh* like a certified reading specialist. When I was finished, thirty minutes later, I half expected a standing ovation but was met with dead silence. Then a kid in the front row raised his hand. His name was Anthony. "Mr. Mooney," he said. "Why do you bother? You know we're retards, right?"

I felt my insides turn out. I thought I was going to throw up as I stood in front of Anthony and all the other kids, like the kids I used to be in the "retard" class with. I wish I could say that I gathered up my guts and transformed myself, then and there, and said, "No. You all aren't dumb. They are wrong about you." I wish I had walked over to the "Reading Is Fundamental" poster and ripped it off the wall. But that's not what happened. I left the class when the bell rang, walked outside, and sat in my car and cried.

I worked with those kids for the rest of my time at LMU. These were the kids that I had shunned when I was younger. They were reflections of myself, and my past, that I had not wanted to see. Now I listened to their stories. Anthony's dad told him that all he could be was a drug dealer. A girl named

Normal Sucks

Heather, who used a wheelchair, had been locked in a closet by some students. They forgot about her until the janitor found her at the end of the day. She had lost her voice yelling for help. A kid named Franklin, who couldn't sit still for even one second, had no hair on his arms from where he had been duct-taped to his desk. Though I didn't have the language yet, I could feel that these were the same processes, ideas, and beliefs that had wounded me. I also realized, because of my relationship with these children, that I believed I was a defective human being. I came to know, to feel, how it was this belief that split me in half, cut me into pieces, and that overcoming my difference would never stitch me up. I needed help, too.

I turned to my sister Kelly, who was always the one in my family, besides my mom, who saw the best in me before I did. Kelly was my closest sibling and my best friend. A theater geek, who, by her own calculations, attended only about half of high school, she and I would ditch school together and ride roller coasters at Magic Mountain.

Kelly gave me the name of a therapist named Susan, an old-school hippie shrink who dressed as if she were a bag of multicolored cotton candy. The first time I met her, Susan had on a periwinkle muumuu, all of the bracelets, necklaces, charms, brooches, and rings the state of New Mexico had to offer, and not just one, but *four* ochre, sage, chartreuse, and Santa Monica blue scarves wrapped around her neck. I had never been to a real shrink before, only sports and school psychologists, so I didn't know what to talk about. She didn't either. She just sat there and smiled at me like a golden retriever puppy.

I wasn't sure how this whole therapy thing worked, and I wasn't sure if Susan knew how this whole therapy thing worked. All the other shrinks I had been forced to see in the past usually jumped right in. The ones I saw for my emotional problems during elementary school asked me a lot of questions about my mom. The sports psychologist told me to visualize various scenes of soccer domination. But Susan just sat there.

"So," I said, "what now?" No words, more smiles. Finally she spoke. "How do you feel?" "Fine," I lied. I don't know, even now, if I knew *how* I felt. I knew that I felt as if my chest were in a vise, and that out of nowhere, every day, I would be subsumed by sadness and hopelessness. "No, you don't," she said. And then Susan did something that I'm sure was not in the recommended course of treatment outlined in the DSM. She got up, walked around her ethically sourced African coffee table, and gave me a hug.

I saw Susan weekly my first year at LMU. It was the best part of my week. Over time, I shared with her my experiences in school. She knew something about these, she told me, and she violated yet another tenet of the shrink bible by telling me about her son's differences and struggles. Susan recommended that I get retested, to which I recoiled in horror. She laughed and told me how it wouldn't be the same as last time. It had helped her son. Susan called the tests an assessment that would provide me with information about my brain, not a diagnosis, and she told me that I could use this assessment to get accommodations.

I recoiled again at the word *accommodations*. I had been on that merry-go-round before and left dizzy and nauseous. To me, *accommodations* had an inherently negative connation to it: one accommodates something he or she doesn't care for all that much, like an in-law's extended visit. Using accommodations in school was stigmatizing. Often, a teacher walked into a class on test day and asked the student with "special needs" who needed extra time to stand up and follow her. Guess how many got up? Zero. In the past, even with teachers like Mr. P who made all sorts of accommodations for me, I felt ashamed and guilty, as if I was cheating. I shook my head at Susan and said, "Nah, I don't need accommodations for my dyslexia. I'll deal with it on my own." She smiled. "You're right," she said. "You don't need accommodations for dyslexia; you need accommodations for *their* dys-teachia."

———

Jake was my best friend in high school. He was a year older than me and drove a Chevy Malibu that had a different color hood from the rest of the car. People made fun of it and him. Jake lived in what my girlfriend and her cheerleading friends called the poor part of town, in a 1960s ranch house with an aboveground pool, which I thought was rad but that others, who had actual pools in the ground, did not. His father was a drunk: nice in the morning, vicious in the afternoon, unconscious at night. We used to skim off the bottles he thought he'd finished. Jake's left foot was bent from birth and twisted, yet he managed to play soccer in what I'm sure was considerable pain that he hid. Jake had shitty teeth like mine because his parents couldn't afford braces or the dentist.

As a kid, Jake had been told he was stupid. Jake worked harder than anyone I knew, including me. We joked that neither of us would live past thirty. We were both wrong. On June 14, 2013, Jake died of cirrhosis of the liver when he was thirty-eight.

So many of the not-normal I have known in my life were filled with, and consumed by, anger. Anger at what? Themselves, of course. The logic of difference as deficiency and pathology turns righteous outrage inward. The logical consequence of being told that you are a problem is to see yourself as *the* problem to be solved, if necessary, through self-destruction. I know my life could have ended like Jake's.

But it did not. While there are many reasons for this, one of them is that I was lucky enough to have multiple people in my life who didn't tell me not to be angry, but told me who and what I should be angry at and what I should do about it. One of these people was named Father Young. I met him at the beginning of my second semester at LMU, when I attended an information session at the English department to help figure out my major. I was at a fork in the road in my education at that time. The previous semester I had mostly hidden my learning differences and tried to just work harder, which wasn't successful. There was one English class, however, where I had managed to have one of the highest grades in the class, only to discover that the final was a handwritten timed essay that would make up over 60 percent of our final grade. I was supposed to be accommodated with the use of a computer but wasn't, so, big surprise, I failed. I was so angry at myself, but also at the fact that a whole year of work was negated by a bullshit test. I did not know what to do with this anger. I figured, what was the point—I was still the dumb kid who was at LMU to major in soccer anyway.

That day, I sat in the back of the room. Then the chair of the department, Father Young—a Jesuit priest and Shakespeare scholar—got up in front of the room. I couldn't take my eyes off him. He spoke about literature and learning and education as if his head were on fire. He reminded me of Mr. P, Mr. R, and the other people who saw something in me before I did. I went up to him afterward and I told him that I might want to be an English major at LMU. But I didn't know if I could do it because of my struggles in school. Father Young looked right at me and said, "Son, some of my best students are people just like you."

I was so inspired by Father Young that I made an appointment with someone from the Office of Student Support. This man was responsible for my accommodations and for helping me navigate the university. During the meeting, I was on cloud nine and sat down across from the man and said, "I think I'm going to be an English major." I told him that it was unfair that I wasn't accommodated for the final last semester and wanted a chance to retake that test. The man looked at me like I was crazy. He reached under his desk and pulled out my file, which was five inches thick. It landed on the table with a thud. He started flipping through it and halfway through he laughed. "English literature," he said. "You can't read, you can't write, you can't spell. You should consider something less intellectual. People like you," he said, "shouldn't even be in college."

I was crushed. Suddenly, I was the kid in the hallway again. The kid hiding in the bathroom again. The kid who was stupid, crazy, and lazy and who should just play soccer again. Later, I went back to Father Young—out of respect for him, so he didn't waste his time—and told him not to worry about the piece of paper I had asked him to sign. I wasn't going to be an English major at LMU. "Why?" he asked. "You were so excited." I told him what had happened. "The dean," I said, "thought I couldn't do it because of my learning disabilities." Father Young was quiet for what seemed like an eternity. Then he looked at me and said in a way that only an old-school Jesuit can, "Well, son, I guess you are just going to have to prove that bastard wrong."

I decided in that moment (and yes, it's true that there are moments in your life of lefts or rights, windows of opportunities for change that open and close) to use the anger that was consuming me to fuel me instead. I became an English major and enrolled in four literature classes. I would do whatever I had to do to prove them wrong. I still felt stupid but I refused to act stupid.

From that day forward, I made myself talk in class when I used to keep my mouth shut. I argued my ideas when I used to capitulate to the smart kids who could spell better. I asked for help. I faxed my papers to my mom and she spell-checked them. I got books on tape, back before digital downloads. The device that played them was so big I had to carry it around in a backpack and plug it into a generator. I used time extensions for exams. This may sound like a small thing, but often in school, how well you know something is secondary to how fast you know it. There is no justification for this. We should not be educating a generation of *Jeopardy!* contestants.

That semester I got a 3.9 GPA.

———

All of us need other people in our lives to push us over the line between what we know we are not and what we think we might be. I found more of those people the summer after my first year in college, at an internship as a union organizer in Denver. For this job, I canvassed neighborhoods to register voters; I picketed employers that violated union contracts; and I spent hours listening to the stories of janitors who were treated as if they were defective and less valuable than others. I was good at this and I cared about it.

I worked with a motley crew of other young people from around the country. Miriam and her brother were from

Tucson, Arizona, and their parents were janitors who had migrated from Mexico for a better life. William, from Clark University, played chess all the time and talked relentlessly about Marxist philosophy and labor politics. These people were different from the ones I knew in Manhattan Beach and at Green Mountain High School and LMU and the kids I spent my life playing soccer with. They didn't care whether I was a good athlete. They liked me for other reasons, and this mattered to me.

When the internship was over, I was asked to stay on full-time as a union organizer for the rest of the summer vacation. That same summer, my club soccer team had advanced to the western regional finals, which was a big deal. I had to choose whether to take the job or play. I couldn't do both. I called Mike, one of my old coaches, to ask his advice. Mike grew up in St. Louis and his parents are Eastern European immigrants. He had the biggest head I had even seen. I know Mike had a hard time in school, thought he was dumb, and soccer became his ticket not just to a better life, but, like me, to a sense of self. On the phone, I asked what he thought I should do, and he didn't hesitate. "Take the job," he said. "You are so much more than a soccer player."

Who someone becomes isn't up to them; it's up to all of us. All of these people pushed me out of the something that I was trying to be into the someone that I was to become. Because of them, I had become a believer in my potential to be someone other than who I was.

———

I got the idea to transfer from LMU from my sister Kelly. She had transferred to UCLA to study acting. When she mentioned the idea to me, I thought she was out of her mind, but she told me that when you transfer, high school grades don't matter. "Your past," she said, "doesn't always determine your future." LMU was not a bad place; it just wasn't *my* place. The people on my soccer team were not bad people; they just weren't *my* people. I wanted to go to one of the "best colleges" with "smart people." Like others before, clawing their way from the outside in, I dreamed of my self-worth in the symbols of power and privilege. When I talked to people about good schools, the Ivy League kept coming up. I did not know what this mythical place was, but it was obvious that if you went there, you were smart, and being smart was what I wanted more than anything.

The Ivy League, apparently, was on the East Coast, because that is where ivy grows. At the time, my brother Billy was living in Connecticut, so I booked a plane ticket and made a plan to visit Yale, Columbia, and the University of Pennsylvania. Why not the others? Cornell was out; someone once said to me that it wasn't a real Ivy League school because it was originally a state agriculture school. (That someone, I'm sure, went to Harvard.) Smart people aside, Dartmouth was just too damn cold, and Harvard and Princeton? I wasn't that delusional. Brown did not make the list because no one mentioned it to me at all until my brother suggested I visit. "It's the weird one," he said.

I drove to Brown first, up I-95, and arrived in Providence by 9:00 a.m. I had never seen a city like that before in my life. Where I grew up, an old building was from 1960; in Providence they had buildings from 1760. I met with the soccer coach first, because while I may be dyslexic, I'm not naive. I was going to work whatever angle I could. After a conversation exclusively about my soccer career, the coach called the admissions office and got me an interview with a harried and disheveled man named Ben. His desk was stacked with vinyl files with brightly colored sticky notes on them. Wow, I thought, look at all the smart people who wanted to go here. I had no chance. Cornell, here I come!

I sat across from Ben and prepared answers to the questions I knew he would ask: How did I do in high school? What were my SAT scores? What AP tests did I take? "What," Ben said in a very serious tone as I held my breath, "is the last book you read for fun?" I exhaled. I had an answer to that one. I had been sneaking books that weren't assigned since my first day at Green Mountain High School and had never stopped. At the time I was reading a book by John Steinbeck. For over an hour we talked about Steinbeck but never once about soccer. I learned that Brown students designed their own education. There were no core requirements, there was no one way to do it. Brown was an education based on passion, purpose, and individual differences.

This was the place for me.

On May 21, 1997, I got a small envelope in the mail from the university. I put this envelope in the trash because good news does not come in small packages. I'm grateful my roommates and I were slobs and let the garbage sit for days. I'm not sure why I picked it out of the trash, but I did, and I know my life would have been radically different if I hadn't.

I had been accepted. I called the admissions office to make sure it wasn't a mistake. "Are you sure?" I asked over and over on the phone. I called the soccer coach and thanked him for getting me in. He laughed. "I'm just as surprised as you are," he said. "Why?" I asked. "The admissions office told me I could have only one player—you or this other guy. I chose the other guy."

I sat on my apartment floor and cried. I called my mom and she screamed. I called Kelly and she cried. I then faxed the admissions letter to the man who told me that people like me shouldn't be in college.

———

I hope you kids have people in your life who see you not just for who you are but for who you can become. I'm sorry for the times that I've taken the parts of you as the whole; the times that I used categories to make sense of you, even as these categories fall apart when held up to you, because I'm not sure what I am without these categories and I'm afraid I don't have it in me yet to hold on to your multitudes. Or mine. Like my mom, I grasp for the safe, for the same, for the acceptable self that will protect you. Don't capitulate to my fear, my limitations, and my attempt to make the bigness of your lives and selves small, clear, and categorical. Resisting normal starts by refusing to hide, refusing to reduce yourself to something—refusing to act normal, ever.

It turned out, that night that you asked me about my dad, you weren't asking an existential question. You were asking a literal one: You did not know who my father was. You did not know his name. You did not even know that I had a dad.

"My dad's name is John, kind of like mine," I said. "But he goes by Greg."

"Where is he?" you asked.

I didn't respond, because I didn't know, and I didn't know what to say. You answered your own question.

"Maybe," you said, "he is hiding."

You weren't kidding. "Maybe he is playing hide-and-seek and one day he will just jump out of the pantry and say 'Surprise!!!! Here I am. I've been here all the time!' Come out, come out, wherever you are, Grandpa Greg. We love you. Hide-and-seek is over."

— VI —

Normal People Suck

All these weirdos, and me getting a little better every day right in the midst of them. I had never known, never even imagined for a heartbeat, that there might be a place for people like us.

—Denis Johnson,
Jesus' Son

Normal is not something to aspire to, it's something to get away from.

—Jodie Foster

One day you asked me if my dyslexia was a disability. We were lying in your bed and I was reading *Wildwood* to you, a six-hundred-page book filled with baroque language written by the lead singer of the indie band The Decemberists. As I read, I stumbled over the ten-dollar words and mispronounced every name, which happens when you read with the right side, which is the "wrong" side, of your brain. I should have, by that point in my life, been able to answer your question without hesitation, seeing how I've spent my entire professional career thinking about ability, disability, and normality. But the thing is, often the more that you think about something, the more complicated it becomes.

At different points in my life, I would have responded to your question with contradictory answers. *Yes* one year. *No* the next. *Yes* one day. *No* another. And in between, a whole bunch of *well, it depends* and *maybes*.

One time when you asked me this question, I turned the tables and asked if *you* thought my differences were disabilities. You had an answer for me in the form of a question. Had I heard the one about the dyslexic who didn't believe in dog?

What *is* a disability? Who are the disabled, and am I one of them? It's a category, of course, that is just one of the many substrata of the normal and not-normal hierarchy. It's a category, however, that can become a person's identity and has the power to shape one's life. There are other categories with the same power, but the learning-disabled one was mine. Are these categories real? Of course not. Of course they are. Both can be true. The categories of abnormality, like disability, are not real, like air, but real like taxes or money.

The question that matters most is: Can someone use these fictional realities based in pathology and stigma to make a better self? I think yes. I did.

I want to tell you how so you can understand, subvert, and use whatever categories you might find yourself in, and then maybe, like I did, you can embrace them to become someone new.

I hope you find a place in your life, filled with people, ideas, and experiences, that cracks you open, breaks you apart, and then gives you the freedom to put yourself back together again, different from when you arrived. I want you to be left stripped of the reflections of you, put on you by me, your mom, your hometown, and by the normal.

———

Brown University, Providence, Rhode Island, in 1997, was that place for me. I didn't seek out Brown to be transformed. To me, Brown was a gold star, the brightest there was, and I wanted it and needed it, because all my stars had been black. I wanted to prove all of them wrong, that I wasn't just not normal but better than normal. Better than my high school girlfriend, her parents, better than those kids in my special education classes. Going to Brown was an act of self-invention and self-creation, but when I arrived, it was not yet an act of self-acceptance.

At this time in my life, I was no longer trying to "pass" as normal. I had an understanding, and tenuous acceptance, of my learning differences. I was, however, determined not to make a big deal about them. I had come a long way since high school, and even LMU. I didn't believe anymore that I was *the* problem, but I knew that I had *a* problem. Or, more like it, problems. I believed these problems inside me were not differences to be proud of, but deficiencies to work around, manage, and cover up as much as possible.

I almost didn't last one day at Brown. My mom and I flew to New York, where we rented a car, taking I-95 up to Providence. It was a hard drive. We spent most of the trip in silence. A week before, two things had happened. One, I learned that my dad had been fired from his job as general counsel of the union where he worked. I'm sure there were many reasons for this, and it had been building for a long time, but the final straw was when he left a cover letter for another job application in the fax machine at his office. He then got a job bagging groceries at the local King Soopers. He had blown himself up once again.

The other thing that happened somehow seemed to bother my mom more than the implosion of her marriage: I had decided *not* to play soccer at Brown. While I had not been admitted as a "designated" athlete, the coach assured me that I would make the team. I spent all summer telling her, and myself, that I was going to play. I decided against it the night before we left for New York, and I told my mom in the car on the way to Providence. She voiced her disapproval with silence.

When we arrived at Brown, we parked off Thayer Street. I was wearing Sambas and a Stussy hoodie. My mom had on JCPenney high-waisted jeans and was rocking a sweet strip-mall perm. We parked our car next to a Saab with a Connecticut license plate. The car looked like a Swedish spaceship unloading a gaggle of Nordic gods. Boat shoes appeared on the sidewalk. There was so much khaki. Patrician vowels filled the air. I struck up a casual conversation with one of the kids getting out of the Saab. He asked me what school I went to. Brown, I said. Wrong answer. He meant what *prep* school had I gone to. Turned out this kid didn't go to Brown but his brother did. *He* went to school "in Cambridge," which is what someone who goes to Harvard says to make you ask them if they go to Harvard.

My mom and I had lunch. Her credit card was declined. I paid with cash. We walked to my dorm room and unpacked. As we did so, I caught a glimpse of my mom, who appeared to be crying. I was stunned; my mom did not cry about her children, and R.E.M. was not playing in the background. But she was definitely crying. When she finished unpacking, she wiped the tears from her cheeks, hugged me, and said, "You don't have to play soccer for me to be proud of you," and then left.

That night, all of the transfer students gathered in the

basement of a freshman dorm called Morris Champlin—otherwise known as MO/CHAMP. Here I was with those kids: the smart ones who raised their hands and got the gold stars. The ones who weren't just normal but better than the rest of us. What had I done? I was a poor white-trash short-bus rider who didn't belong here. This was a big mistake. These people would find out that I wasn't supposed to be here.

We went around the room and shared where we'd transferred from and what we did the summer before Brown. This got off to a terrible start. The first kid had worked at Goldman Sachs for the summer. Good for her. The next kid had transferred from Princeton and worked at the National Institutes of Health. The next kid had transferred from Harvard and was on a short list for a Nobel Prize. I was out of there.

I decided I would go to my old standby and run to the bathroom right before my turn. Then the next guy stood up, and he was quite a sight to see. Purple hair spiked like a porcupine, bike chains around his wrists as bracelets, and overalls splattered with paint. When he spoke he sounded as if he were chewing on a shoe. He said that his name was David Cole, he was from Hanover, New Hampshire, and he'd transferred from Landmark College—a two-year college for kids with learning disabilities and attention disorders. And he'd worked construction that summer. That, I said to myself, is my boy right there. I couldn't believe that he had outed himself in front of all these smart people. There would be no hiding in the bathroom that night.

After the introductions, and much to my dismay, the ice-breakers continued. We were handed a list of anonymous "fun" facts that we were supposed to match with other transfer students. I beelined past the Goldman Sachs girl right to David and introduced myself. "My name's Dave," he said, as he ran his finger down the list of fun facts to the middle of the page. "I got it," he said. "Circus performer." I didn't get the joke and said very seriously, "No, I played Division One soccer." "No way!" he shouted. "Don't buy that for a second." "You?" I said. "Investment banker," he deadpanned. "Now," he said, waving his hands wildly, "tell me something else. Tell me something really interesting."

I told Dave that I was dyslexic and had not learned to read until I was twelve years old. Dave was the first person I had ever told this to. Then he told me his story: high-school dropout, struggled with substance abuse, graduated from a two-year college, an artist. I was speechless. "What's your fact?" I asked him. His fact was that he learned to weld when he was eleven years old. He laughed and said, "Looks like I learned to weld before you learned to read!" He continued. "Your thing is cool, too." "Cool?" "Yeah. Are you kidding? The dyslexic brain kicks ass."

I went home that night and sat in my dorm room alone and thought about what Dave had said. It was like he had told me that a circle was a square. It was unfathomable to me that this thing, my brain, my disability, my deficit, could be anything other than a problem to be fixed, a deficiency to be denied, a part of myself to hide. Cool hair aside, I knew Dave Cole was full of shit.

To claim that my brain, my deficiency, "kicked ass" is to argue that forms of differences considered pathological are not inherently deficient. Back when I was in college, I could not see this. I was then, as so many still are, snared in the normal net, caught in a sea of scientific research that "proved" that dyslexia and ADHD were "neurobiological-based deficits and disabilities." Years of school failure proved this research right: there was something wrong with me. And there were clear examples of what types of humans were better than me: the kids in the smart reading group, the ones who could sit still, the ones who were normal when I was not. Didn't all of this prove that they were right about me? About us?

But. Here I was, in a place they said I could never be. I still spelled at a third-grade level. I still couldn't sit still. I still had the same problems they said I had, but *I* wasn't a problem anymore. Was it possible that they were all wrong about me?

One night, a week into my first semester at Brown, I met Dave at his dorm room to go out to dinner. He was late and was still in the shower. I sat on his bed, waiting, and listened to his stream-of-consciousness patter, the ADHD version of singing in the shower: *Did you know that Robert Rauschenberg was dyslexic? Hanover is sixty-five miles from the border of Canada. That girl Sara looks like a frog. Where should we go to dinner? Not Kebab and Curry again. You should go to AA. Good coffee. We should write a book.*

The stream abruptly stopped. Dave walked out mid-shower, naked, water pooling around him, and said, "Yeah, we should write a book," as if it was the most logical thing in the world for an ADHD high-school dropout and dyslexic who did not learn to read until he was twelve years old to write a book. I laughed at him. He got back in the shower and picked up midstream as if nothing had happened. There was always another idea waiting for Dave in the shower.

Two weeks later, I had a dream about school that I had often. One moment, I am in the hallway, because I couldn't sit still in class, talking with the janitor; the next I am checking the stalls in the bathroom to make sure no one else is in there; then a long corridor; then I am back in the stupid reading group, stumbling over every word as I read out loud in front of my class. I woke up at 1:30 a.m. and called Dave. I knew he didn't sleep much either.

"Yeah," I said over the phone. "We should write a book."

———

Brown was a strange place. Founded by outcasts from the American colonies, populated in the 1950s by sons (daughters went to its women's college, Pembroke) of the wealthy who had been rejected from Harvard and Yale, the college was taken over by the counterculture in the sixties to become what it is today: the weird Ivy where there are no core requirements and students take whatever, whenever they want. An education based on the individual.

Dave and I did start to work on a book, and this book became the center of my education. I would ultimately do three-fourths of my "classes" at Brown in some form of independent study supporting this project. I had three mentors during this time: Susan, Robert, and Graciella. These people scared the shit out of me and taught me that people who scare you have the most to teach you.

Susan was a postmodern literature professor who, I was sure, read Derrida in French and called Judith Butler "Saint Judith." I met Susan my first semester at Brown, when I enrolled in her advanced literary theory class because that, we all know, is what smart English majors do. I remember my first day in her class vividly. It was my first class at Brown. I was terrified but prepared. I had purchased two packs of colored pens, five pads of sticky notes, two mechanical pencils, three erasers, one graphing calculator, and a Trapper Keeper–like contraption that my mom had bought me from Wal-Mart, which appeared to be the only one on campus. Clearly, I was ready.

I was forty-five minutes early to class. I sat in the front row, dead center. Susan walked in and had rattlesnake-curly hair, wore all black, and when class began spoke in a whisper, which just made her sound louder. On the board she wrote *Jacques Derrida* and everyone nodded. She then proceeded to speak a foreign language that everyone in the room but me appeared to understand: poststructuralism, the signified and signifier, differ and differing, and something about the post-modern gaze. My eyes glazed over, which, I learned later, was not what she meant.

I felt then that this whole Ivy League English major thing wasn't for me.

Susan then turned to the class and asked, "Why does all this matter?" Good question. A frenzy of hands shot up and long-winded answers spewed forth in that same foreign language that I began to suspect many were speaking without understanding what they were saying. Susan politely listened and then said that this matters because language shapes the world, gives us categories, and if we understand how this happens, you can deconstruct yourself and "build someone new." Now this was a language that I needed to know.

Susan became my advisor at Brown and my friend. She introduced me to the idea that many of the things that we consider natural and self-evident always have been and always will be "social constructs." She continued to speak a language that I struggled to understand but felt was relevant to my life. Susan was also the first person, other than Dave, who I told about the book idea. I told her that the book was about how Dave and I had overcome our learning and school challenges to be successful. She smiled and said to me that the book sounded interesting and important but might be about much more than I thought.

Dave and I met every Wednesday night from nine to midnight in the basement of MO/CHAMP to work on our book. That's not what we were really doing. Sure, we acted like we were writing a book. We brainstormed about chapters and "the market." But really we were telling our stories to each other, and in doing so, to ourselves. Dave was much further along with this than I was. He had transferred from a school that was specifically for students with learning and attention differences. For one of Dave's final exams, he broke into his professor's office and created an immersive art installation based on the content of the class. He got an A. It was the kind of place where no one passed as normal because being not normal was the norm.

That wasn't the case for me. I didn't yet know where my story started, so Dave gave me a little interview:

Who and *how* look the same?

Check.

Can't tell the difference between *house* and *horse*?

Check.

Best friends with the janitor?

Check.

Hid in the bathroom to escape reading out loud?

Check.

Learned how to read with your eyes closed?

Check.

Found a special talent (soccer) to compensate?

Check.

Felt in school and still feel that you are stupid, crazy, lazy, and defective?

Check.

I sat in the halogen light of the MO/CHAMP basement speechless. How could Dave know my story before I did? "You are not the only one with a brain like yours, you know," he said. In that basement, over months, we researched the history and science of learning and attention disorders. Once I got past the titles of most of these studies—okay, of all these studies—I actually found the science made me feel better. I struggled with reading and writing not because I was stupid but because of "left hemisphere deficits." I always lost my car keys, not because I was lazy or intentionally disorganized, but due to "frontal lobe impairments."

Dave and I were not the only ones to find safe harbor from the moralization of differences. So many of what we now call neurodiversities were moralized before they were pathologized. The kid who couldn't read was dumb, the one who couldn't sit still was bad, and the one who didn't make eye contact willfully defiant. The science named these as real "problems," not character flaws. Negative labels aside, I knew, sitting with Dave in MO/CHAMP, that being dyslexic and ADD was a whole hell of lot better than being stupid, crazy, and lazy.

The medical model freed us "not normals" from the tyranny of moralizations with the gift of pathology—but it wasn't that simple, of course. Another mentor of mine, then and now, named Robert pushed me to think more deeply about this issue. Robert ran the Swearer Center for Public Service, but like many at Brown this job description meant nothing. Robert was a painter, a writer, a queer activist and theorist, and he was an adopted, sexually nonnormative Marxist who had a passion for colonial architecture and MTV.

I met Robert when I applied for a job running a tutoring program at his center. We quickly became friends as he shared with me ideas about the social construction, and pathologizing, of sexuality and the movements of the 1960s, 1970s, and 1980s that revolted against what he called "compulsory heterosexuality." I'll be the first to admit that I found many/most of Robert's ideas deeply challenging. I did not know any openly gay soccer players, nor did my parents hold openly progressive ideas about sexuality. Once, I told my mom that in another life I would be an interior designer, and she asked me if I was a fag. I wasn't totally sure what, if anything, this all had to do with me.

One morning over coffee, Robert told me that I *had* to read two seminal books by Alfred Kinsey called *Sexual Behavior in the Human Male* and *Sexual Behavior in the Human Female*. I had a few questions for Robert: One, did these books have pictures? And two, what the hell did books like these have to do with my experience and project? Robert explained to me that beginning in the late 1940s Kinsey conducted the largest study of human sexuality in history. Unlike past studies of sexuality, which focused on "abnormal" behavior, Kinsey studied "the more typical of the population." He interviewed one hundred thousand men and women, asking each more than three hundred to five hundred questions over multiple hours. Nothing was off limits in these interviews. This study concluded that the vast majority of sexual behavior considered "abnormal" was in fact quite typical, quite normal. "The living world," Kinsey wrote, "is a continuum in each and every one of its aspects."

If the world is a continuum in all its forms, maybe, Robert said, it is wrong and is an act of culture, not nature, when some parts of this continuum are grouped, categorized, and labeled as sick and others not. Maybe, he suggested, we are all on a continuum of ability and disability of some sorts and just don't know it yet.

———

Dave eventually moved off campus to an industrial artist's loft on the south side of Providence. We worked on the book there, amid Dave's collections of industrial stools, old tools, medical objects, gas station signs, used books, vintage school supplies, and so many other ready-made art objects Dave had pulled out of dumpsters or rescued from thrift stores.

That loft is still one of the most beautiful places I've been in my life.

For our research Dave and I read a book called *ADHD and the Nature of Self-Control* by a clinical neurologist named Russell Barkley. Barkley was then and remains one of the leading experts on ADHD in the world. The book, as is the case with Barkley's academic research, was filled with long passages, and even bigger words, describing the deficiencies, defects, and deficits of the ADHD brain. One day, I arrived to write and found Dave pacing around, reading this book and muttering to himself. After a few minutes of this, he threw it down, walked over to his computer, typed furiously, and printed out a new cover for it that read: *A Very Bad Book by a Very Bad Man*.

At that point Dave and I had helped each other tell a new, more complicated story about ourselves. Was Dave really someone that had a "deficit" of attention when often he spent days making art without leaving his studio, eating, or sleeping? "You have a learning *disability*?" Dave asked me one day, when I recited, from memory, verbatim, something we had talked about weeks before. Were we really "pathologically" hyperactive when we were working on a book *and* taking a full load of classes, when most of our peers were, uh, not? In that loft, with and because of each other, the objectiveness, the naturalness, the inevitability of the categories applied to us began to fall apart.

———

A woman named Graciella nudged us to take the questions we were asking ourselves (Is disability a fact in the world? Is disability a medical category or a minority identity? Are differences valuable?) even further. Graciella was the chair of Brown's education department. Born in Mexico, raised in New York City, she was a radical education activist who believed special education, and all labels, should be abolished. She recommended (i.e., made me read) books that talked about disability not as a medical reality, but, as she called it, a social construct.

These books were the opposite of the research studies Dave and I were reading. They included *The Politics of Disablement* by Michael Oliver, *The Rejected Body* by Susan Wendell, *Extraordinary Bodies* by Rosemarie Garland Thomson, and many other texts that rejected the medical model of disability. Instead they argued for what these scholars, advocates, and social theorists called the "social model," which posits that disability is caused by the way society is organized, its structure, values, and attitudes, rather than by a person's limitations, impairments, and differences.

I didn't buy it. At that point in my life, I believed that I *had* a learning disability and this was a biological fact, not something anyone made up or constructed. Graciella and I argued over this. One morning, she told me a story about a little girl named Carolina, who wasn't supposed to be alive. She was born with her umbilical cord wrapped around her neck and was stuck in the birth canal for five minutes without oxygen to her brain. She survived but was paralyzed, with the exception of one eye, and had to breathe through a respirator and have a full-time health aide. When she was asked what she would change about her life if she had a magic wand, she blinked out a response through her assisted communication device: "I wish people didn't stare at me."

———

Dave Cole and I sold our book idea to Simon & Schuster in the fall of 1998. That same semester, I took a poetry class with a well-known poet. The grade for this class would be based on one long paper, written on a poet of our choosing. Throughout the year we also wrote in-class responses to poems that were ungraded. A week after I submitted my final paper, I was called into the poet's office. She had my weekly, handwritten responses laid out next to my final, typed paper. She accused me of plagiarizing my final paper because "the person who wrote these horrible responses could never have written something like this." At that point at Brown, I had a 4.0 as an English major and had sold a book to a major publishing house. But I was once again being wrongfully accused of cheating. For a moment I felt like that kid back in the sixth grade, but then I asked myself, Was I really the problem? No. Well-known poet aside, I thought of what my mom would do and then let loose, for the first time, my inner cursing Mickey Mouse, and advocated for myself, shattered glass and all.

———

As Dave and I were working on the book, I was also volunteering at a local elementary school, where I worked, for a time, with a kid named William. Before William was assigned to me, I had a sit-down with one of his special education teachers. William, she told me, was mentally retarded—the official label that the state of Rhode Island used to describe people who experience intellectual disabilities. She told me that William couldn't read, couldn't write, barely spoke, and couldn't dress himself. After this briefing, the teacher walked me to William's classroom. He was big for his age, with a lumbering gait. At that moment, he was standing quietly in the back of the room and appeared to be watching the birds outside the window. I introduced myself. He didn't speak or shake my hand. He pointed to the birds.

At 8:15 a bell rang and the rest of William's class started to walk in and find their seats. William didn't. He stood in the back watching whatever was in his world outside the window. I asked William if he wanted to find his seat. He didn't answer, just turned toward the row of desks and started to lumber toward one of the seats in the back row. William stopped, however, at the first seat that was occupied by a little boy; William wouldn't move. "Let's keep going," I said to William. "Time to sit down." William bent down and gave the kid a hug. "Best part of my day," the kid said. I watched William for the next five minutes as he walked from desk to desk, stopping at each one and giving each kid a hug, fist pound, or high five. I learned later that William did this every day, to every kid, in every class. William, I realized, wasn't mentally retarded. He had the emotional IQ of Gandhi. He had the spiritual intelligence of Jesus.

I sat outside of William's school, and I thought about him, and I thought about me. Give me something I care about, and there was not a deficit of attention but hyper attention. I can't spell, but I could talk better than anyone I knew at Brown. I could see patterns on the soccer field others never spotted. I was the builder, the talker, the explorer. People spent so much time focusing on what was wrong with me that for so long, I couldn't see what was right.

I left that school asking myself, What do we miss—what do we willfully ignore, misunderstand, fail to know—about ourselves and others when we make difference the problem? Everything, I think.

———

One night in the loft, Dave asked me if I could, would I get rid of my learning disabilities? As a kid at LMU, and on the first day of Brown, I would have answered hell yes. But now I was confused. Here Dave and I were, with the same brains as before, but we were succeeding instead of struggling. Was I still learning disabled?

My past looked different to me. I had always been so ashamed of not being able to sit still, but why was that so important? I had been told that reading was the most important thing a human being could do, but it isn't. At Pennekamp and beyond, a set of cultural values created an environment that worked for some brains and bodies, but not all, or even most. Being compliant was conflated with being good. Reading was confused with smart, normal confused with right, and not normal mistaken for wrong. In that environment, and so many others, Dave and I were treated as if we were less than and we had grown to see ourselves that way.

I had come to realize that one is not born a person with a disability. One is *made* into one. Normality, ability, disability are not features or facts inside a human being but a relationship *between* the reality of human variability and the social environment that surrounds, constrains, enables, or disables differences. Ability and disability are contextual. The dominant ideas, attitudes, and customs of any society determine the perception of which bodies, brains, and humans are called right and wrong.

My answer to Dave was no.

———

"You should be proud of your differences," Robert often said to me. Proud? No one I had ever met like me, not even Dave, was proud. Accepting, maybe. Open, sure. But never proud. "You," he said, "should go to a local elementary school and tell your story with some kids like you, and I'll bet *they'll* be proud."

I decided to call Robert's bluff and arranged to speak to a group at a local school. My speech was terrible; a forty-five-minute rant about the failures of traditional education, the marginalization of people with differences, and the social construction of disability delivered to . . . first graders. When this was over, I saw a sea of bored faces and promptly headed to the exit. But before I could leave, a six-year-old boy came up to me. He thanked for me coming and told me that he had a hard time in school and didn't feel so stupid anymore, and then he gave me a hug. Robert had been right.

I went back to my dorm room and called Dave. "We should create a program where students like us from Brown mentor elementary students like us." Dave laughed hysterically. "That's the worst idea I've ever heard. People like us? Mentors?" And he hung up the phone. A second later he called back: "I'm in."

We called this program Project Eye-to-Eye. We recruited five elementary school children from Fox Point Elementary School and five college students, one from the Rhode Island School of Design and the rest from Brown, as mentors. It was a motley crew: Dave Cole (who was late to every single meeting); Sarah, who attended RISD and had been referred as part of her probation for a public art project in Boston where she painted the entrance to the T as a vagina; another Dave who had been a professional magician; a woman named Patrica who made avant-garde films that lasted twenty-four hours; and finally, a guy named Brent who had long hair down to his waist, a beard, looked like Jesus, and during his interview at Harvard, had pretended his head had caught on fire, rolled around on the floor, and screamed in pain. Brent did not get into Harvard, but he did get into Brown, which says a lot about Brown. Perfect mentors, these were not.

The first day of the program, we had no idea what the hell we were doing. It was the epitome of "fake it until you make it." The plan was for each of us to share our school experience with one student and then do an art project. We paired off and each began to talk one-on-one to a kid. I was with a kid named Eric. After twenty minutes of talking, I took a break to see how it was going with the other groups. The first crew was quite a sight to see. Brent was talking with a third grader named Jimmy, who had every label known to the shrinks: ADHD, OCD, ODD, and a whole bunch yet to be discovered (give 'em time). Jimmy was a hurting kid. He was so terrified of school, his teacher told us, that he hid under his bed in the morning and begged his grandma not to make him go.

Once I got within five feet of Brent and Jimmy, I heard Brent—who was usually fairly soft-spoken—screaming at Jimmy. "Jimmy," he yelled at the top of his voice, wild-eyed, arms flailing, "if you learn one thing today, you have to learn that normal people . . . suck—they *suck*, Jimmy!" Now, that's an awkward conversation. My heart stopped. I didn't know what to do or say in the moment, so I pretended I did not hear one of my mentors cursing at a third grader. Later that night, though, I called Brent on the phone and yelled at him. *How could you say that to a kid? What were you thinking, saying that in a school?* Brent didn't say a word as I berated him until I was done and he said, "It's true. Normal people do suck." And he hung up the phone.

I hoped that it would be water under the bridge. No principal had been present, no teacher had been there, so we could forget the whole episode. But I was wrong. The next morning I got a call from the principal of Fox Point Elementary School. She respectfully summoned me to her office to discuss what had transpired the day before. I drove to the school and ran through my mind all the ways that I could apologize for screwing this kid up. To confirm my fears, when I got to the principal's office, not only was the principal there, but Jimmy's grandmother was, too. The moment I walked into that room Jimmy's grandmother stood up and pointed at me, and asked, "What did you do to my grandson?" "I didn't do anything," I said. "It was that Brent guy." Jesus Christ or not, he was going right under the grandma bus.

Jimmy's grandmother had tears in her eyes. "For three years," she said, "my grandson has hidden under his bed before school. For three years, from our house to school he cries and begs me to turn around. But today Jimmy was up early waiting in the car ready to go to school. What the hell did you do to my grandson?!" I looked at her and said, "Well. It was my good friend Brent." For the first time in Jimmy's life, he had been told that he wasn't broken, he wasn't the problem, and that helped him get out of bed and face a world that wasn't made for him.

———

I graduated from Brown University on May 25, 2000, with an honors degree in English literature. *Learning Outside the Lines*, the book I coauthored with Dave while at Brown, was published in September. Eye-to-Eye would grow into a national organization.

But you boys need to know that the most important thing that happened to me at Brown, the thing that changed my life, wasn't the book, or Eye-to-Eye, or Dave, or Robert, or Graciella, but meeting your mom. I met her in a playwriting class, and the moment I saw her, I was stunned. It took me a month to talk to her. During that time, I followed her, from a distance, every day after class, trying to get up the nerve. I finally did, and we started emailing. I was terrified and spent hours composing and spell-checking and rereading my four-line emails. I couldn't let her know, not yet, maybe ever.

Our first date was at a coffee shop. Our second, I picked her up at her dorm room for dinner. I peeked my head in and panicked. Your mom's walls were a shrine to the New York Knicks, generally, but specifically to Patrick Ewing, the Knicks' seven-foot-tall center. I thought this was the end of the line, because I obviously didn't have what she needed. She noticed the look on my face, laughed it off, and then proceeded to tell me more about the Knicks and the NBA than most sports announcers could possibly know. She knew the starting lineup for every team. This was a passion, one of many, that spiraled out of her like concentric circles that could not be squared.

Becky, my Patrick Ewing–adoring, John Starks–worshipping, West African–dancing, fluent in Spanish and American Sign Language, tough little New Yorker. I was in love.

I eventually told her about my learning differences. On our one-month anniversary I wrote her a note littered with misspellings. She didn't laugh. Or crumple it up. She still has it in her wallet today. Years later, after we were engaged, I asked her if she was sure she wanted to get married, because if we had kids, odds were one of them would be like me. "A kid like you," she said, "is exactly what I want."

No one has scared me more than your mom. No one has taught me more than your mom. No one, in my life, has loved me as I was more than her, either.

———

Disability theorist Tobin Siebers wrote that to protest, to resist, to heal is to reject the false claims made about you and to criticize the existing state of knowledge that made these claims. He wrote, "Individuals in protest against unjust treatment begin to develop theories that oppose the majority opinion, not only about themselves, but about the nature of the society that supports the pejorative behavior." Resisting normal requires reframing who and what we call the problem. It wasn't the ADD or the dyslexia that disabled me. What disabled me were limitations not in myself, but within the environment.

I know now that this is what limited me: the passive

learning experience where kids sit at a desk most of the day; a narrow definition of intelligence conflated with reading and other right-brain skills; and a medicalization of differences that reduced my brain to a set of deficits and ignored the strengths that go hand in hand with many brain differences.

I want you know that I did not and do not *have* a disability, as it is common to say, but *experienced* disability in environments that could not accommodate and embrace my differences. What disabled me was the way that my differences were treated in an environment that was hostile to some bodies and brains and not to others. Ability, disability, and abnormality are not facts in the world but social constructs we create as a society.

It is what Foucault called a "transactional reality"—something created by public policy, professional power, and everything in between. Just like normal, *not* normal isn't a thing in the world that was discovered—it doesn't live inside people's bodies and minds. It is not personal misfortune or individual defect. It is the product of a normalizing and disabling social environment built for the normal at the expense of everyone who is not. This is the problem.

— VII —

The New Normal

People who are defined by a variant set of norms commit a kind of social suicide when they begin to measure the worth of their relations and their way of life by the yardstick of normalcy.

—Michael Warner,
The Trouble with Normal

There are forms of oppression and domination which become invisible—the new normal.

—Michel Foucault

One night, you asked me, "Who made the rules?" You were six years old and in kindergarten, and rules, and who made them, and their fairness, were all that mattered. It was 9:00 p.m. on a Tuesday, we had gotten up that morning at 5:00 a.m., and this was clearly a teachable moment that I was not seizing.

"Rules are important," I said with a dismissive yawn. "Now go back to bed."

This tried-and-true parental platitude did not satisfy. "No, Dad!" you yelled. "I want to know who made the rules!" You seemed really upset, and I wondered, Did something happen at school? You extended both hands and then yelled at the top of your lungs, "Who made the rules that women had to wear tops at the beach?" It was clear that you had been giving this social issue a lot of thought. "What?" I asked. "Did some man just came into city hall one day and say, *Hey, you women, I don't want to see your boobs anymore.*" I was speechless. You were not—and you continued. "But what if men had penises on their faces? What then? Would they have to wear a special face mask to go outside that made them look like Pinocchio? No. That wouldn't happen. So I want to know. Who made the rules about what is normal? And can they be made different?"

———

The answer to the first part of this question is easy. The world is not built for the different, but for the same, and its architects are the few, the powerful.

The second question is harder: Can these judges be overruled? I know that normal has always been—and still is—a shape-shifter. Normal is not a fact in the world but a historically contingent construct we've created that has proven adaptive, malleable, and changeable. One century, pink and purple are the normal colors for boys, the next century for girls. One era, the idealized body type is large and voluptuous, the next skeletal. Normal can and does change. I have pointed to these examples of normal's shape-shifting as evidence of the hypocrisy of normality. One day it's this, the next day it's that. I used to believe, and argue, that this shape-shifting is evidence that we can create a *new* normal that includes more humans and more ways of being essentially making difference . . . normal. But I don't believe this anymore. I know now that while new norms are possible, as normal changes, its power over us stays the same. I've come to believe that normal, the word, the idea, and the values it represents, can't be used, or appropriated, or repurposed but must be rejected, and I want to tell you why.

———

I didn't always believe that normal had to be rejected. In fact, I like so many others who have found themselves on the wrong side of normal, I coveted normality. I had been ashamed of my differences and thought that passing as normal would make things better. It didn't. I came to embrace my learning differences as real deficits and disorders. And, then finally, toward the end of my time at college, I came to reframe these disorders as social constructs, and the problem wasn't in me but in the *environment*. I had hoped that this would be the end of it: if my so-called disabilities were social constructs that weren't real, then I was normal, wasn't I? At that point in my life, I still wanted to be normal, because not normal has always been less than, and to claim normal is an attempt to reclaim oneself.

But it doesn't work that way. This act of reclaiming is really an act of self-negation. Every society has struggled to integrate and accept difference. Social systems have either corrected difference to make it disappear or included, even tolerated, certain types of differences as normal—differences that don't require changes to the world of the same. Just declaring a love of diversity and renaming certain differences as normal, while the world stays the same, is to tell kids like me that we are all different and then set us loose in a social environment that tells us, compels us to stop being different.

I experienced this hypocrisy after graduating from Brown and fumbling my way to the life that I live now. When I graduated, I moved to New York City. I had, in retrospect, no viable life plan, though at the time, I thought I had totally Tony Robbins-ed the shit out of my life. I found an apartment on Twenty-Ninth Street between Park and Madison Avenues. It was a one-thousand-square-foot two-bedroom, two-bath apartment for $1,500 a month. For New York City, this was too good to be true, which meant that it was too good to be true. The apartment was above an Indian restaurant, and it came with an additional roommate in the form of a curry-loving rat the size of a small cat that lived in a hole in my bedroom inches from where I slept. This rat came out at night, so I blocked its hole with my copy of James Joyce's *Ulysses*. The rat was not a Joyce fan and proceeded to gnaw through the seven-hundred-page tome. The apartment building also happened to be between police precincts, and as a result, was the largest and most trafficked thoroughfare for prostitutes in New York City at the time.

Professionally, I thought I would move to New York, my book would be published, it would be a bestseller, and I would make tons of money and be showered with offers to write another. I also thought that this success would open the floodgates of funding for Eye-to-Eye to become a national nonprofit organization.

Turned out, there were a lot of writers and nonprofits in a city of eight million, and no one was clambering to fund us. I cold-called foundations to ask for grants, was rejected and told to please not call again. By August, I was pretty much out of money. I felt myself disappearing again; maybe the dyslexic brain didn't kick as much ass as Dave thought. Maybe I had just fooled them all and the game was up. I had used success at Brown to fill up my chart with the gold stars that I never had before, and it had made me feel better. If you derive your sense of worth from success, then there is always another gold star for you to chase, and then another and another. My dad asked me that summer what my plan was if the whole writer/nonprofit thing didn't work out. I told him I would go to law school—a gold star if there ever was one.

I decided to take matters into my own hands, and I spent the summer trolling chat rooms for learning and attention issues. I would directly email people, which, it turned out, was kind of a stalker thing to do. A few brave souls, mostly moms of kids like me, however, responded. I told them that I would come to speak in their community, for free, if they set up the presentations and let me sleep on their floor. This publicity "strategy" worked, in a way, because I would spend the next year of my life traveling around the country, supported by a few brave moms who responded to my misspelled emails, sleeping on their couches or floors, or in their child's bed (sans child) and giving talks about my book and my experiences to whoever would listen.

It was because of one of these moms, a woman named Leah, that I came to give my first official speech on my "book tour" about my experiences in school to a small group of sixth graders in special education at a school in San Diego. These sixth graders in San Diego were the first audience to be subjected to my emerging very professional public-speaking style: think stream-of-consciousness rants containing things that should not be said in front of children. I remember this presentation vividly because at some point, I decided to talk about a psychologist named Martin Seligman who studied living organisms in pain, and told the kids about one of Seligman's most infamous experiments. For this experiment,

Seligman built a cage, which was divided in half. Both sides of the cage were electrified. He then put a dog in the cage, and the experiment consisted of shocking the dog from both sides as it tried to escape, increasing the frequency and intensity until there was no safe place for the animal to go.

The teacher had a look of horror on her face. Still, I continued, and I told the kids how this experiment reminded me of my time in school. The teacher audibly gasped. I explained the analogy: I'd show up in the morning and my foot started bouncing. *Jonathan, hallway.* First shock. Next class was reading. Grab *See Spot Run* and hear it for the rest of the day from all the other kids. *Jonathan, go back to your retarded reading group.* Next shock. Next is recess where the last person picked in the classroom is often the last picked on the playground—that's me. Another shock. Then it's reading out loud time, and I hide in the bathroom. Another shock. Then I go home, and my dad starts up with *What's wrong with you, Jonathan?* Last shock. All the shockers are on. I have nowhere to hide.

By the time I had finished this story, the teacher was gesticulating wildly for me to stop. I did not. Instead, I asked the students what did they think happened to the dog in the cage when it hurts all the time? I still remember the silence this question was answered with. No one moved. No one made eye contact. No one breathed. The story of the dog meant something to these kids. Finally, a kid in the front row raised his hand. He told me his name was Miles. He had blue eyes and a blond-tipped afro with purple streaks. His backpack was stitched together with safety pins, duct tape, and punk rock band patches. He looked me in the eye and said, "If the dog had opposable thumbs and could get ahold of a lighter, it would smoke some dope."

Everyone laughed. Miles didn't laugh. "After the dog was stoned," he said, "he would kill himself." No one laughed. The room filled with the kind of silence that comes after someone shares a truth that wasn't supposed to be shared. I stood in this silence, until I couldn't anymore, and then I left the room and cried in the hallway.

———

We can call differences normal all we want, but the reality is that despite all our talk about differences, and the hope for a more expansive idea of normal—a new normal—the judges of normality have not given up on finding new ways, which are really just the same old ways, of squaring the round peg. From that day on, I've heard from thousands of people who feel hopeless and less than, like Miles did. I've thought a lot about these stories over the years. I've told my own story. But I still don't understand them. I still feel shame, because what happened to me wasn't all that big a deal in the scope of things, right? That, at least, was what I was made to feel. I struggled with reading, spelling, sitting still. People tried to help me with these things. So why did I not want to live by the time I was twelve? Was I weak? Was I a coward? I've thought all this about myself and more. And yet, I'm not alone.

Despite the rhetoric of diversity, the ranks of the not normal have continued to grow. Our social environments, schools, places of work, and communities have grown more restrictive, not less, and as a result more people than ever are labeled as having brain and body disorders. Each new edition of the *Diagnostic Statistical Manual*, published by the American Psychiatric Association, adds, on average, 25 percent more "disorders" than the last. Special education is the fastest growing form of education in the nation, and traits such as shyness that used to be considered differences are now disorders. And, of course, the institutions that generate abnormality continue to make more and more money as the remediation and pharmaceutical industrial complex hums along. I guess in that sense, we actually do have a new normal and that new normal is that more humans than at any other time in history have been labeled not normal.

Brain and body differences are still consistently treated as deficiencies to be cured. Here's a stunning example: In the fall of 2008, New York University's Child Study Center, a child and adolescent mental health research institute, launched a national PSA campaign to raise awareness of childhood mental health issues. The campaign consisted of more than two hundred ads on billboards, construction sites, and kiosks in New York City in addition to ads in national newspapers, magazines, and websites. The first one that I saw in *New York* magazine was a handwritten note, akin to those created by hostage takers, which read, *We are in possession of your son. We are making him squirm + fidget until he is a detriment to himself and those around him. Ignore this + your kid will pay.* Signed ADHD. Another note, from Autism, read, *We have your son. We will make sure he will no longer be able to care for himself or interact socially as long as he lives.* The one from Asperger's syndrome read, *We have your son. We are destroying his ability for social interaction and driving him into a life of complete isolation. It's up to you now.* All told, there were six other "ransom notes" that had the same message about differences: *This is only the beginning. . . . Ignore this and your kid will pay.*

———

I've come to believe that it is impossible to claim difference as normal without negating differences. While coming to this belief was a long process over many years, it started when I met a kid named Jack. After that first speaking gig in San Diego, I spent six months sleeping on people's floors and speaking for free everywhere I was asked. It wasn't until the spring that I gave my first paid presentation. This trip was organized by a woman named Jill, who was one of the few brave souls who had responded to my summer of spam and taken it upon herself to arrange a series of speaking engagements for me.

I had offered to do all of the talks for free, but Jill found a school that was willing to pay me $250 to speak to a group of students. Jackpot! I was out of money and paid for the bus to the airport in change. Jill picked me up at the airport and we drove directly to the school. In the parking lot, Jill told me that the school I was speaking at was "very traditional" and then added, in a third-generation Midwest accent that would make any Packer fan proud, "But, golly, are they nice!"

I was greeted by the principal. He shook my hand and said, "Wow, are we excited to have you here! You are so inspiring, and it is so important for students to know that they can overcome their problems." The principal gave me a tour of the school. One classroom, however, caught my eye. As we walked by, I thought I had seen a student in the back, jumping up and down, in what appeared to be some sort of box. I asked the principal if we could stop for a minute and check out this classroom. "Sure!" he said enthusiastically. "This is one of my best teachers. Good with kids like you!"

I hadn't been hallucinating. In the back of the room, there was a three-foot-tall box made out of cheap plywood book-shelves, and in this box was a student. This, I had not seen before. I turned to the principal. "Hey, man. What's up with the box?" I asked, with all due respect, pointing to the back of the room. "Oh, that's Jack. He's a lot like you and can't sit still," the principal said, without a hint of irony.

I wasn't sure if this guy was kidding or not (it's hard to tell with people from the Midwest sometimes). "Are you serious?" I asked. "You have a kid named Jack in a box in the back of a room in your school?" I asked. "Yep," he said nonchalantly. I was speechless and before I could ask if they had other kids, in other forms of stigmatizing, life-altering confinement, I was taken into another room for my speech.

As I waited for the kids to arrive, I sat on a little red chair, processing what I had just seen. I felt nauseous. They had put a kid named Jack in a box. This was just wrong. At 1:25 the bell rang, and students filed into the room and, sure enough, in walked Jack. He found a seat in the back of the room, put his head down, bounced his feet, drummed his pencils, and did not look at me.

The teacher got up to introduce me and silenced the room with a cultlike hand gesture, followed by an elaborate clapping routine. Once the kids quieted down, she said, "Jonathan used to be like you. He had learning and behavior problems, but overcame his dyslexia through hard work. Let's welcome Jonathan!"

I walked slowly to the front of the room. I wasn't usually nervous before speaking, but that day my throat tightened and my hands were moist with sweat. Something was wrong. My story was being used to tell these kids that their differences were deficiencies that they had to overcome with hard, tireless work. Here, differences would be tolerated, even celebrated, as long as they did not demand the school to change. And here I was being called to present *my* difference to these kids, in a way that reinforced the idea that we should all be exactly the same.

While I didn't have the language at the time, I felt in that moment that I was being celebrated, to paraphrase David Mitchell and Sharon Snyder, because of my ability to approximate a "specific expectation of normalcy." As they wrote, this type of "inclusion" tolerates difference as long as these differences do not demand excessive change from any institution, which only reaffirms, and strengthens, a narrow set of norms for belonging and acceptance. In other words, different can be normal as long as normal gets to stay the same.

This wasn't inspiring but shaming. I looked at Jack in the back of the room and knew that he needed to hear another message. ADD was not his problem. The box was the problem. I had always felt the cosmic injustice of normalcy even though I did not understand it. The normals have always needed us, used us, because without us there is no them. This is wrong.

I walked up to the podium, thanked the school for having me, and then, channeling my shrink from LMU, said, "I didn't overcome dyslexia but dys-teachia. School sucks if you are different and that's not your problem. It's theirs." I don't remember what else I said that day. But I do remember that after my talk, Jack gave me a hug. And I wasn't paid.

———

Normal, even if it's new, is always contingent on something and someone being *not*. To have an inside there always has to be an outside. For me, after college, as is the case with too many people, that outside was *other* people with "significant" cognitive and physical differences. For a long time, I held on to the idea that I wasn't like "those people." My differences were socially constructed, differences turned into disabilities by a limited and flawed definition of learning and the normal human brain. *Those* people, regardless of the environment they found themselves in, were really, intrinsically, not-normal disabled brains and bodies.

I wasn't alone in this narrow and bigoted belief. Many in the learning differences community intentionally distance themselves from the broader disability community for the same reasons. To climb up from the bottom of the bell curve, you need someone below you to step on. To be on the right side of normal, there has to be, is always, someone on the wrong side.

A young man named Henry whom I met that year traveling was on this wrong side. I met Henry at the PEAK Parent Center's annual Conference on Inclusion Education in Denver, Colorado. This was my first professional keynote address, with a podium and a microphone, in a ballroom with more than one thousand people and proper lighting. Becoming a professional speaker was never a plan of mine. I just kept speaking, wherever I was asked, got better at it, and learned not to curse so much in front of children. But the PEAK conference was still a big jump from the presentations I had been doing in fluorescently lit cafeterias to twelve kids after PTA meetings. This doesn't mean, however, that I was in any way *professionally* prepared for this event. I wasn't into doing much prep at the time. I pretty much just showed up and went off the cuff, so I knew little about PEAK and did not take the time to learn more. I simply figured it was a conference for parents and teachers of students with learning and attention differences.

The executive director of PEAK, Barb, was going to meet

me at the hotel with her son, Henry, with whom she said I would have a lot in common. Henry, she told me, had many of the same experiences that I did, had gone to college against the odds like I had, and co-taught a class on education at a local college. When I arrived I didn't see anyone there to greet me, so I walked to the front desk to check in. I was then tapped on the shoulder by Barb, who had recognized me. She was with a young man who was in what appeared to be a motorized hospital bed–wheelchair hybrid. "So great to meet you," Barb said. "This is my son, Henry."

I looked around the hotel to see whom Barb was pointing at and then realized that she was pointing at the guy in the bed–wheelchair contraption next to her. I looked at Henry. He was paralyzed with the exception of one eye, breathed out of a respirator, had various other tubes protruding from his prone body, and communicated through a Morse code–like blinking system translated by Barb. This guy was nothing like me, and Barb was clearly delusional. "What the hell?" Barb said to me, because I was staring. "You've never seen a college teacher who craps in a bag and blinks to talk? What kind of school is Brown, anyway! Come on, let's show you around."

I spent two days with Barb and Henry. Barb reminded me so much of my mom. Foul-mouthed, hard, relentless. She heard many of the same things about her son that my mom had heard about me. Endless deficit-based IEP meetings, relentless low expectations about her son's future, and discrimination because of his differences. Henry shared his experiences with me, too, and they were similar to mine—but for different reasons. He was made fun of, he was sent to special education, his talents were ignored, the value of his mind was questioned, and he was made to feel less than human because he wasn't normal.

During my time at the conference, "those people" that I had kept out of *my* new normal to affirm my own normality shared their stories of discrimination, struggle, and pain with me. These echoed and reflected my experiences. Billy, a kid with Tourette's, was taped to his chair in school; Mariana, who used a wheelchair, was fired from her job because she was late to work . . . at an office with no ramp; Sherry, who had Down syndrome, was told, like me at one point, that all she could do for a living was flip burgers. The more people with differences I met, the more I saw it wasn't them. It was us. It wasn't the autism but the bullying; it wasn't the mobility impairment but the segregation and shame of the short bus. Much like I had concluded about myself at Brown, it wasn't the difference that disabled these people, but the way the difference was treated.

My time at PEAK ended with, of all things, a dance party. The party was held in a bland corporate ballroom. Pink streamers dangled from the ceiling, and strobe lights illuminated the corners. Everyone from the conference was there dressed to kill and ready to party. Some wore formal gowns. One guy had on a tux. Others took a more West Village Halloween parade approach: cowboys and cowgirls in wheelchairs, sexy vampires on ventilators, and one dyslexic

Humpty Dumpty that I'm still trying to figure out. The dee-jay was a young woman with Down syndrome who was very excited to be there and/or extremely caffeinated and deeply committed to GETTING THIS PARTY STARTED!!!!!

This was the prom for us SPED kids.

I stood in the back of the room with Henry and Barb, reluctant to join the celebrating. "Want to dance?" Henry asked. "No, thanks," I said as the deejay implored everyone to GET THEIR BOOTIES ON THE DANCE FLOOR AND MAKE MY DAY!! "I don't much like dancing," I lied. I actually love dancing, but I was too embarrassed to dance in public because of something that happened in middle school. When I was in seventh grade, my favorite song in the world was "Ice Ice Baby" by Vanilla Ice. I loved this song so much that not only did I memorize every single line, but I also made up an elaborate dance routine. Okay, elaborate is a slight exaggeration. The routine consisted entirely of varia-tions on the running man: fast running man one verse, slow running man the next, side running man another, other side running man again, and then superspeed backward running man for the chorus. I had done this dance in public only one time in my life, at the seventh-grade social, where I was laughed at, and I never felt comfortable dancing again.

I didn't share this story with Henry, but somehow he knew how I was feeling. "Don't worry about looking silly," he said/blinked. "You can't possibly be any weirder than us weir-dos." I looked out at the dance floor and saw that Henry was quite right. *Soul Train* it was not, unless I missed the episode where the train was ditched for a short bus. On the dance floor, a young man with intellectual disabilities did what only can be described as the dying worm, a bunch of folks in wheelchairs were doing some type of conga line, and a kid with multiple differences seemed to have beat me to the running man routine with the added twist of actually *running* around the dance floor between bursts of the Roger Rabbit. I looked at Henry and then at Barb and said, "I guess you are right. Difference is normal here." Barb laughed and said, "Different is just different here."

Henry rolled out to the center of the dance floor. I followed. You never know what you'll learn from a person who can't talk. I had been holding on to the dream of normality for so long. When I had been diagnosed all those years back in elementary school and walked out of the shrink's office, I knew I was not normal, and whatever normal was, I wanted to be it. I had spent much of my life trying to be it, hiding what didn't fit its parameters, fighting against myself, capitulating to its narrowness, defining my worth through its narrow aperture. But with these weirdos, I wasn't so sure anymore. Becoming normal had been conflated with happiness and worth. That side of the line was better. But maybe it wasn't. These people were not trying to be normal, or claiming normality, and because of that, they were free to be different. Free to be themselves. Eventually I got up the courage to ask the deejay to play my song. She did, and I found a spot on the dance floor and ran, in place, like my life depended on it, going nowhere, and no one laughed.

———

Barb was right. We can't make difference normal because normal doesn't exist. It has been and always will be a statistical fiction. I'm happy to report that on this point, even the judges of normality agree with me. After the whole Norma-and-Normman debacle, the judges of normality called it quits. They realized, when they couldn't find an actual normal human, that normal had to go. No more normal versus not, and no more squaring the round peg.

Kidding.

The judges of normality have not given up their quest. After Norma and Normman, they soldiered on with more sophisticated tools to determine, with scientific rigor, what is a normal human. And what have they discovered?

In the 1950s, the US Department of Agriculture set out, at the behest of the National Mail Order Association of America, to develop an industry-wide standard for clothing sizes based on the "normal" body. More than fifteen thousand (white, of course) women were measured. What they discovered was that the body measurements of the "average women are of limited usefulness. The nation's women vary far too much in size to be properly fitted by garments made for the average women." There was no normal woman's body because human bodies comes in a "bewildering variety of shapes and sizes."

In 1990, the Human Genome Project launched with the goal of determining the typical human genome. This required identifying and mapping all the genes that made up the human genome from both a physical and a functional standpoint. However, given the fact that no two people's DNA is alike, mapping the "human genome" involved sequencing the genes of a small number of individuals and then assembling these together to get a composite or mosaic for each chromosome. When the project concluded in 2010, the "normal" human genome discovered by these initiatives was in fact an aggregation and an abstraction, normal just like Norma and Normman. Turns out, as the science writer Matt Ridley wrote, "variation is an inherent and integral part of the human—or indeed any—genome."

In July 2009, President Obama launched the Human Connectome Project, a five-year $50 million initiative sponsored by the National Institutes of Health. The goal of this project was to build a "network map" of the normal healthy human brain. To date, a consortium of universities has scanned the brains of more than twelve hundred "healthy" people between the ages of twenty-one and thirty-five. These scans have failed to identify any common, typical, or normal structure for a healthy brain. According to Tom Insel, the former NIH project director, there is great variation among normal healthy brains, and "it's not so categorical as: this is normal, this is abnormal."

In 2011, the World Health Organization conducted the world's largest study of disability, ability, and typical functioning. The study showed that more than one billion people in the world live with some form of disability and another 200 million will experience considerable impairments in typical functioning as they age. Another study showed that 40 percent of people have experienced an auditory hallucination; half of all people will experience a mental health challenge; 40 percent are neurodiverse; and, as a result of aging, 50 percent of humanity will experience physical impairments at some point in their lives. We are all only temporarily able bodies and minds. Statistically, what have been labeled mental and physical "abnormalities" or disabilities are essential to the human condition, are in fact *the* human condition.

———

You get the joke by now, I'm sure. And it's not funny. Every time anyone in human history has ever tried to find the normal human, all they discover is the reality of human variability and difference. To claim differences as normal is a negation of this reality. We cannot expand normal circumferences and create a new normal, because normal is always contingent on what is not and only exists when a line is drawn on the vast continuum of human variation separating the normal from the not, us from them, and all of us from the reality of ourselves.

More than ever, I believe we must reject normal as a word, a value system, and as a way to live. Because in our twenty-first-century digital surveillance economy, normal still keeps everyone in their right place. As David Mitchell and Sharon Snyder wrote, in this dynamic, we are sold products through the heightening of our imperfections, which are framed as pathologies deviating from narrow norms of health, which creates yet another normal to chase. These new norms power our Fitbits to track our changing deviations in the endless quest for bodily improvement, and curated social networks like Instagram create unreachable standards of image and practice. More than ever, we are surrounded by numbers that become algorithms that tell us what is normal, and in telling us, nudge us away from difference, toward sameness. This sameness, too, is constantly changing, which feeds a never-ending cycle of normalization. In this game, being normal isn't a destination, but a horizon that you'll never reach, but will continue to reach for as it recedes, *because* it recedes, even further into the distance.

Normal has always been a code word for the few and the powerful justifying their power and their privilege as a fact in the world rather than a position gained on the backs of the bodies and minds deemed below them. Enough already.

As Kinsey wrote, "The terms normal and abnormal have no place in scientific thinking." They have no place in our lives, in your life. Difference is not normal, which has always been and always will be a statistical fiction. Differences are true. Difference is essential. Difference is a fact in the world. In fact, it is the world.

— VIII —

Normal People Are People You Don't Know Very Well

The *presumptuousness* of it all. On the one hand, the Aristotelian, perhaps evolutionary need to put everything into categories . . . on the other, the need to pay homage to the transitive, the flight, the great soup of being in which we actually live.

—Maggie Nelson,
The Argonauts

If we are to achieve a richer culture, rich in contrasting values, we must recognize the whole gamut of human potentialities, and so weave a less arbitrary social fabric, one in which each diverse human gift will find a fitting place.

—Margaret Mead,
Sex and Temperament

One night, as I was writing this letter to you, you asked me to "pinkie promise" that I would go see my dad. I hadn't seen him, or spoken to him, in five years. I told you that it wasn't as simple as just picking up the phone and calling him.

"Why?" you asked.

"My dad wasn't a normal dad," I said.

"Normal?" you said, eyebrows arching, voice rising, eyes alight with the rush of catching adult inconstancy. "Normal? I thought normal sucks, Dad?" you said, with tween glee for my hypocrisy. "Can't you forgive him? We all make mistakes sometimes."

I responded with silence.

"Pinkie promise me that you'll see him this week," you demanded.

"I'll text him," I said.

"No, see him," you persisted.

"I'll call him," I said.

"No, see him," you said, extending your pinkie.

"Maybe," I said, without pinkie promising a thing.

You turned away from me and faced your bedroom wall. "Imagine if *we* said that about you, and what if he dies, and then you go to his funeral and see him only when he can't say anything to you? How would you feel then?" I didn't answer you, because the truth was ugly: how to explain to you, my son, that my dad had been a mess for so long that I probably wouldn't feel anything at all?

I want you to know that difference is not something to be overcome, tolerated, accommodated, remediated, or normed, but a fact of human existence to be celebrated as valuable in and of itself. That's easy to say, isn't it? And it would make a damn good bumper sticker, but, as you rightfully pointed out, when it comes to my dad and his differences, often the things that are easiest to say are the hardest to do.

Every society has struggled and failed to integrate the reality of difference. Every society has struggled with the hot mess of human embodiment. I've come to believe that we are in denial of this fact because we have yet to value our variations, our fallibility, and our vulnerability as what *constitutes* our humanity. Every person is caught up in this struggle and I am no different, because what is most true is sometimes hardest to believe.

———

I wish I could say that, after meeting Miles, Henry, and Jack, I learned what I needed to know and the rest of my early twenties were all good—but they weren't. I thought traveling the country telling my "success" story would be enough. That day with Jack was far from the last time that I heard that I had overcome my disabilities. I was once introduced to a group of students as someone who "used to be like them" but was "normal" now. My story was constantly contorted as an "overcoming" story, which I reinforced sometimes and resisted other times. I had hoped and thought that success—an Ivy League degree, a published book, winning awards—would be enough. It wasn't.

I know now that at that point in my life I was in between knowing that normality was a dead end and not knowing what should take its place. I had spent so much of my life trying to prove those judges of normality wrong, and in doing so, had proved their case against me—us—right. I was done with that.

During this time in my life, I came across a beautiful essay called "Escape from Shame" by a disability rights activist named Tammy S. Thompson. Tammy was born three months premature and weighed two pounds and twelve ounces. Her life was saved, and she was legally blind due to retinal damage. In college she was diagnosed with hydrocephalus, a condition where excess cerebrospinal fluid builds up in the brain. It almost killed her.

Her experience of disability was very different from mine, but when I read her essay, I was stunned by how similar our emotional response to being different was. Her words: "I've spent many years on a mission to cancel out my disability by frantically stacking up achievements, hoping that someday I would find that final, magic accomplishment which would absolve me of the sin of being disabled. Loneliness and longing for fulfillment have been the constant threads in my life, motivating countless escape attempts. I guess I thought that if I were successful enough, I'd escape from the 'less than' feeling that quivers in my guts."

I realized, for the first time, reading her words, that I too had tried to cancel out my difference by stacking up achievements and hoping that if I was successful enough, I wouldn't feel *less than* anymore. I had stitched myself back together with thin thread, and it was fraying and I was falling apart again. I felt myself disappearing into the corners of rooms and still didn't know if I had a future or a place in the world. I found myself alone, drunk in shitty hotel rooms, far away from home on speaking engagements, and there were days when I couldn't get out of bed.

One night in the fall of 2001, I met an old friend from LMU at a bar in the West Village in New York City. The last thing I remember is him saying to me that I had changed so much from back then. How different I was. How successful I was. Then nothing. I woke up the next morning, back in my apartment, my clothes covered in blood. My drinking was out of hand, and that night I drank way too much, but this was just a symptom of something deeper. That wound within myself that I had tried to stitch up with success and normality was still there, bleeding. I knew that it was time to get help.

In the fall of 2001, I started to see a shrink again. His name was Alex and I chose him because of his exceptional collection of African totems and his very impressive beard. Unlike Susan, my therapist from LMU, Alex was by the book. I can count on one hand the number of words he said to me in our first session together. He had, however, mastered the art of the thoughtful nod, followed by the best delivered *tell me more* that I've heard in my life. At first I thought that he often would fall asleep during our sessions, but he fooled me by turning the inevitable on-the-verge-of-sleep head jerk into his thoughtful nod, followed, masterly, by a well-timed *tell me more*.

In one session, Alex asked me about my school experiences; he responded by *uh-huh*-ing helpfully and *tell me more*-ing at the right moments. After I was done, he was quiet for a long time and closed his eyes, and I thought, *Now I've caught you sleeping, you shrink bastard!* I leaned forward, prepared to snap my fingers in his face, when he opened his eyes and said, "Have you ever considered that you are a valuable human being, not despite your differences but because of them?"

———

That sentence cost me fifty dollars a word, but it was worth every penny. At that point in my life, I had come to understand my dyslexia as a difference that was disabled by a school environment made for a narrow type of learning, but I had yet to claim my differences as valuable. This had left me adrift. There was power in the social model for disability I had learned, but it did not create a space for me to value differences as anything but value-neutral. In the social models I learned about at Brown, these were "impairments," or deficits, that became disabilities. But what if my brain was more than that? What if, as Alex suggested, these were real differences that caused impairments and challenges, of course, but were also *valuable* in some way that I did not yet know?

I had tiptoed into this territory back at Brown. Dave and I tried to convince ourselves that learning and attention differences had an upside, only to read yet another study about our disorders and our problems. For every funded research project exploring the strengths of brain differences, there were at least ten other studies, often funded by pharmaceutical companies, that perpetuated the idea of brain differences as disorders—and very little has changed since then.

After college, I had spoken about the need to reframe learning disabilities as valuable differences, only to be rebuked by professionals, and at times the LD/ADHD community, for minimizing these as not "real" disabilities. There continues to be a cognitive dissonance around claiming disability and differences as valuable, and this dissonance is a part of the larger system of normalization. People with differences get services in school, their struggles are recognized, but only if they are willing to pathologize themselves, emphasize their problems, downplay their strengths, and claim differences as deficiencies.

As I traveled the country after college, however, I saw more and more anecdotal evidence of the value of different brains and bodies everywhere I went. I met kids who couldn't read but could draw, kids who couldn't write neatly but spoke beautifully, kids who couldn't sit still but could hustle, and kids who couldn't pay attention but could dream and invent. In every state and town I visited, "those" kids handed me comics strips, drawings, told me jokes, and shared science projects and experiments that won national competitions. I met parents, teachers, and professionals who pulled me aside and whispered about the gifts, talents, and strengths of kids with differences. I learned about, and then from, people like Ned Hallowell, Oliver Sacks, Temple Grandin, and other leaders of an emerging movement of advocates, psychologists, educators, and neuroscientists that believed in and advocated for the value of differences.

During that year, I also began to understand the intrinsic value of my differences. After one of my talks I was asked by a kid what kind of job I had. I told him that I didn't have a "real" job and that I was going to apply to law school and become a lawyer. "That sucks," he said. "Too much reading. You should keep speaking. You're good at that. My dad's a lawyer and he's a dick!" That kid was right—I was good at speaking. This may sound trite, but I had never realized this about myself before. I had always been told that I talked too much or too loud, and was told to be quiet. In school, my speaking ability was not valued or considered a strength or gift, but discouraged, dismissed, and punished. But there I was, being asked to talk *more*.

While there are many things I thought I should do to make other people such as my dad happy, to continue proving them wrong through traditional success, there was only one thing that I was meant to do and that's to talk. I wanted to use my speaking to advocate for change. I decided that year that speaking as a form of advocacy could be my life. I was good at it, not despite my dyslexia but perhaps because of it.

For much of my life, however, there was only anecdotal evidence to support the belief that so-called brain disorders were in fact differences that had value in the world. The stories of LD artists, ADHD entrepreneurs, computer programmers with autism, and others thriving not despite but because of their differences were often buried under an avalanche of deficit-based research and dismissed as delusional mothers' wishful thinking, people in denial about their "problems," or irresponsible professionals. It turns out these parents weren't delusional. These teachers were not naive. And these radical professionals were hardly unprofessional. These people were right about how wrong the world has been about brain differences. As documented in two important books, *Neurodiversity* by Thomas Armstrong and *The Power of Different* by Gail Saltz, MD, over the past fifteen years a growing number of interdisciplinary researchers have documented the strengths of a continuum of brain differences and validated the idea that these differences are an important form of human neurodiversity.

This research has fundamentally complicated and challenged the dominant cultural and scientific view of autism. This is only right seeing as how the term *neurodiversity* was coined in the late 1990s by Judy Singer, an Australian social scientist on the autism spectrum, in her sociology honors thesis. The idea of neurodiversity was then shared widely by an autistic advocate named Jim Sinclair, who was a principal early organizer of the international online autism community. Jim did not learn to speak until he was twelve and was one of the first to publicly challenge the pathology model in a 1993 speech called "Don't Mourn for Us," in which he beautifully argued that "there's no normal child hidden behind the autism. Autism is a way of being."

Research has finally caught up with Jim and others from his movement and shown that autism is not just a way of being, but a way of being that adds value to the world. It is clear that many people with autism have profound strengths in pattern recognition, systemizing, and attention to detail. As reported by Armstrong and Saltz, in randomized and peer-reviewed studies, individuals on the autism spectrum are better than neurotypical control groups at speed multiplication, identification of prime numbers, calendar calculations, perspective drawing, factual memory, and block design tests.

These cognitive strengths lead to what one researcher calls "hyper-systemizations." As Mary Ann Winter-Messiers wrote in her paper "From Tarantulas to Toilet Brushes" (which must be the best title ever for an academic paper), 90 percent of children on the autistic continuum have special interests in systems as diverse as "deep-fat fryers, the passenger list of the *Titanic*, waist measurements, the livery of Great Western trains, Rommel's desert wars, paper bags, light and darkness, toilet brushes, globes and maps, yellow pencils, oil paintings of trains, photocopiers, the World War II propeller plane Hawker Hurricane, industrial fans, elevators, dust, or shoes."

This "strong systemizing," according to a Kings College researcher, "is a way of explaining the non-social features of autism: narrow interests, repetitive behavior, resistance to change, and need for sameness." While this predisposition to systemizing causes clear challenges, it also has real world advantages, as Gail Saltz wrote in *The Power of Different*. A study published in the journal *Biological Psychiatry* by researchers at Stanford found that children with ASD displayed greater mathematical problem-solving ability than a control group. Fathers and grandfathers of autistics are twice as likely to work in math-related fields. Autistic Daniel Tammet in 2004, at age twenty-five, set the European record for memorizing and reciting 22,514 digits of pi in five hours and nine minutes. He knows English, Finnish, French, German, Lithuanian, Esperanto, Spanish, Romanian, and Welsh, and he learned Icelandic in a week.

In 2013, German computer software giant SAP, seeking innovation that "comes from the edges," launched a recruitment drive for software testers specifically seeking autistic people. A recent case study at SAP found that individuals with ASD supported by its Autism at Work Program helped develop a technical fix worth an estimated $40 million in savings.

It is not just the autism community that has benefited from new research on brain differences. As early as the 1980s, parents and a small group of professionals challenged the medical deficit model that was applied to brains like mine and advocated instead for a learning and attention *diversity* model. How did that go? Remember my file from elementary school through college? There was zero mention of anything *positive* about my brain. Nevertheless, as Dr. Gail Saltz documents in *The Power of Different*, a growing body of evidence arising out of the field of neurodiversity has revealed that there is not only a very wide range of variability in the human brain, but that many of these variations, while causing difficulties in particular areas such as reading and executive functioning, also bring *capabilities* in other areas.

The first brain scan of someone with language-based learning disabilities occurred in 1997 at the MIND Institute, and these scans continue to this day. These researchers are looking to identify the brain deficits that lead to learning disorders. These studies found that, especially in individuals with language-based learning differences, there were deficits in the left hemisphere of the brain, which is used to read and process language. They also found—confirmed in numerous follow-up brain scans at Yale University and elsewhere—that people with learning differences had larger right hemispheres, the part of the brain responsible for a wide range of visual and spatial tasks. I'm not sure why these findings were ignored, but I can only imagine that the deficit/disorder orientation (and funding source) colored how those findings were interpreted. If you are a hammer, every problem is a nail.

Neurodiversity researchers from multiple institutions

around the world have also found that people with learning differences have what is called "holistic perception," which encompasses a tendency to see the big picture in situations, stronger peripheral vision, higher than average visual-spatial skills, strengths in deciphering patterns, and the ability to "interact with their auditory environment while drawing upon their wider spatial attention," enabling them to recognize patterns others cannot see. As a result, there is a much higher percentage of students with learning differences enrolled in elite art programs compared to the general population, and more than 35 percent of entrepreneurs have some form of language-based learning differences.

What about attention differences? Based on both the science of neurodiversity and creativity, the judges of normality might as well rename ADD Artistic Deficit Disorder and start diagnosing the accountants of the world, because attention differences are clearly linked to creativity and originality. A ten-year study commissioned by the National Institute of Mental Health showed that the frontal lobes of individuals labeled ADHD are 3 to 4 percent smaller than those of a control group. This area of the brain is known in the scientific community as the "where the hell are my car keys and why haven't I paid my taxes?" hemisphere. Deficits in this area lead to some very real neurological-based challenges such as impulsivity, hyperactivity, distractibility, and poor self-regulation.

These very "deficits," however, are also the same cognitive traits that correlate with creativity and complex problem solving. Bonnie Cramond, the director of the Torrance Center for Creative Studies and Talent Development at the University of Georgia, has found a strong correlation between brain structure and temperament in people labeled ADHD and others who are considered creative. According to an article in *Frontiers in Psychology*, impulsivity, hyperactivity, and creativity are all linked. Creative individuals are impulsive and, as a result, tend to act on their ideas rather than just talk about them. Many people with attention differences are considered inattentive daydreamers, but according to a study from Berkeley, daydreaming is linked to complex problem solving. Bottom line: people with ADD have higher levels of creative thinking than those without.

Finally, the science of neurodiversity has advanced a more complex, nuanced, and positive view of what have historically been considered mental health disorders. Depression, anxiety, bipolar disorder, and even forms of schizophrenia have been linked to advantageous and positive cognitive traits. This research does not in any way ignore, or negate, the very real challenges and suffering associated with these brain disorders but does offer a deeper view of human experiences that have been pathologized.

As Gail Saltz wrote, "multiple studies show that people who experience high levels of anxiety more accurately assess emotions in others, better predict outcomes, are more attentive to details than control groups, and perform to a higher standard at work." In fact, a high degree of anxiety correlates positively with intelligence in people. The higher the levels of anxiety, the more likely a person is to have a high IQ. Genetic research suggests that intelligence may have co-evolved with worry in humans, which means I'd hire an accountant or lawyer with an anxiety disorder over one without any day of the week.

Numerous studies have found that forms of depression are accompanied by above-average IQ and creativity. Bipolar disorder is also linked with various forms of creativity and artistic temperament. Nancy Andreasen, a neuroscientist and neuropsychiatrist at the University of Iowa, conducted a decade-long study of writers at the renowned Iowa Writers' Workshop and found that 80 percent of these writers had some mental illness, compared to 30 percent of the control group.

Even a genetic disposition to schizophrenia—what many would consider unequivocally a "disorder" with little advantage—is associated with creativity and achievement. As Armstrong wrote, "In studies of the entire population of Iceland, people who scored at the top of their class in academic subjects, especially mathematics, or who showed more creativity, were more likely to have first-degree relatives who had experienced psychosis than those who were less successful or creative."

Taken as a whole, the research on neurodiversity is a profound rebuke to our collective illusion of sameness—and the systems of normalization that make this dream a nightmare for many of us. This body of research shows that a constellation of brain differences are not only correlated with, but directly lead to, a range of thinking patterns and cognitive skills like creativity, problem solving, intelligence, and innovation that have made humanity's progress possible. As Harvey Blume wrote in an article in *The Atlantic*, "Neurodiversity may be every bit as crucial for the human race as biodiversity is for life in general."

Back in the day—I mean *way* back in the day—somewhere on the savanna there were two groups of prehumans. In one group, a member was moody, withdrawn, and prone to outbursts of sadness, but he could draw. Another was hyperactive and frankly a pain in the ass, always losing keys to the cave, pacing back and forth at dinner, and never sitting still, but she could hunt. Yet another was antisocial and never made eye contact, but, as Temple Grandin said, while the others where chitchatting around the fire, she figured out how a stone could be a spear. And there was the nervous one who couldn't sleep but kept everyone on time and figured out which berries not to eat. Finally, there was the one who could talk—okay, grunt—better than the rest, who negotiated with the other tribes and told the best stories.

Somewhere on that savanna, there was another group in which the members were all the same. Which group do you think survived? We did.

———

It is important to know, though, that these findings and accomplishments capture only a fraction of the value of difference, and the list is incomplete—and if it is left incomplete, it will be in the service of the judges of normality. To celebrate *some* form of difference as valuable because that form is associated with positive outcomes trains us to justify the worth of these differences pragmatically. This means we think they are valuable because they bestow upon some of us not-normal special powers. This logic values deviations from the normal only if they are made up for by an awakening of new and seemingly magical abilities. This is an old story: the not normal overcome abnormality by displaying some special "ability" and become twice-as-good normal. The circle gets bigger. But to have an inside, you still have to have an outside. And my hierarchy, the terms in which I valued differences, left out a lot of humans so that I could get in.

I began to understand the limitations of how I valued differences as I met more people after college with differences very different from mine: people with Down syndrome, nonverbal autism, or cerebral palsy, people who were deaf or blind, and so many others who did not fit the hierarchy I had constructed. These people were not successful artists, entrepreneurs, or innovators, and they were not begging for entry into the circle of normal. Rather, they were insisting on their own value, without caveats—not if they could draw, or make jokes, or go to Brown—but as they were.

At some point after I started seeing Alex the therapist, I was on an airplane flying to somewhere, and I was rereading a book I had picked up at Brown called *The Rejected Body*. There were a number of passages highlighted, with question marks next to them. I stopped on one and read it, then reread it:

People with disabilities have experiences, by virtue of their disabilities, which non-disabled people do not have, and which are sources of knowledge that is not directly accessible to non-disabled people.

Then I read another passage:

What would it mean, then, in practice, to value disabilities as differences? . . . It would mean seeking out and respecting the knowledge and perspectives of people with disabilities. It would mean being willing to learn about and respect ways of being and forms of consciousness that are unfamiliar.

I was stunned by these passages. I know that Henry and so many others I had met did not fit in my hierarchy. In excluding them, I was affirming a narrow view of which humans are of value and, by doing so, valuing only the parts of myself that fit this norm. I had believed that to be okay, I had to become a carbon copy of what I was told I was not. But proving "them" wrong, collecting gold stars, being better than normal, better than others in the SPED room, hadn't put me back together. Maybe those bodies and brains that had been demeaned—that I had demeaned—had something to teach me, to teach all of us. Maybe these short-bus riders, who, at times, were told their lives weren't worth living, had something to teach me about living a better life. I decided to find out.

———

On March 15, 2003, with the little money I had saved from speaking gigs, I bought a short school bus. Yep, the kind that takes kids enrolled in special education to school. I called my dad and told him that I would not be going to law school or any other graduate school.

Instead, my plan was to drive cross-country and listen to and learn from the experiences of those who lived beyond normal. In June, I flew from New York, where I lived, to Los Angeles to pick up the bus. I traveled for six months, drove forty-five thousand miles, and visited forty-eight states, all the while interviewing people with different brains and bodies.

I got off my short bus in October 2003, but my journey to learn from those who ride continues. Over many years of being an advocate for different brains and bodies, I've come to believe, as Sharon Snyder and David Mitchell wrote, that the experience of living on the other side of normal allows someone to inhabit the world as an "innovative, embodied being, rather than merely as a devalued social construct or, worse, a victim of oppression."

These lives are valuable not because they have overcome, not for their compensatory abilities, not because they can approximate normalcy—but because they challenge normality as a prerequisite to personhood, self-worth, and human dignity. They are proof that there is no single way to be human. They are valuable because they have something to teach us about what it means to be human and how to live life as it is, not how it should be.

I am forty-one as I write this, and my journey on the short bus happened many years ago, but I turn to what I've learned from "those" people who rode it more than any other time in my life. I've always taken refuge in my body and its ability, because my mind wasn't able, and I am ashamed to admit, even now, that I'm scared of who I will be, that I won't be valued, or loved, when it fails.

In the mornings, I feel myself seeping out, only to hold myself together with relentless exercise and artificial-hair-restoration research. I catch myself dreaming of that old sameness, seduced by what Instagram and the wellness/medical/entertainment industrial complex tells me is the abnormality of my fallibility. I think maybe I should get a tattoo or freeze the fat or, better yet, get a tattoo on the place where I froze the fat. In these moments, I turn to what I learned from the people I've known in my life who have lived the reality of human differences.

I learned from a man named Bill how wrong we are about what makes us human. Bill, a man with multiple physical limitations, picked me up from the Fairbanks Airport in Alaska in 2009 and drove me five hundred miles to Anchorage using only his *mouth*, through one of the largest wildfires in state history. After the ride, Bill said that "Descartes got it wrong. 'I think therefore I am' is bullshit. Our bodies and minds are vulnerable, fallible, variable, therefore we are."

Bill was right about how we've got the human all wrong.

Difference and disability are not an exception to the rule of human life, but are the rule of embodiment and constitute our humanity.

I also learned from Mary, a girl with Down syndrome, when I asked her how she felt about having an aide in school, and she said, "Silly Jonathan, don't you know people need other people?" We are not independent but interdependent. We are not those mythical, independent creatures of the social contract, but dependent, divergent, and vulnerable bodies and minds that, as Tobin Siebers wrote, "rely on others for survival." Mutual care is a basic need of all humans, and dependence on others is what makes us human.

I've learned that hands can speak, listening is reading, talking is writing, and that human intelligence and ability are not one thing, but many. Intelligence is not singular but multiple, and it is bigger, stranger, and more wonderful than we've all been led to believe. It is a crime every time we ask ourselves how smart a person is, instead of asking ourselves what makes that person smart.

I've learned that we are all temporarily able bodies and minds moving in and out of states of ability and disability every day of our lives. Sooner or later we all fall off the center of the bell curve. Our bodies, minds, and lives change. The goal posts surrounding what is normal for us will move, and we will lose our own normality if we ever thought we had it. This fact of our lives requires a new ethical, moral, and political philosophy. It requires a new way to live, a new social system. For all of us, normal is just temporary, and we are only visiting—for a fleeting moment—the center of the bell curve.

I've learned from Henri-Jacques Stiker that our love for the same has led to a world built for the same. Space and time, social roles, styles of communications: all are designed for the normal—at the expense and exclusion of the different. This must change, not because it is the right thing to do for "those" people, but because it is the right thing to do for all people.

I've learned that the disability rights movement asks a fundamental question that any just society must answer: What kind of world would we build if we awoke from the dream of the same and embraced the reality of difference? It is a movement that targets the politics of the same in all its forms, for all its victims, and imagines a right to be different for all of us. At the center of this movement are the bodies and minds that are different and have been dehumanized, demeaned, and marginalized because of their difference.

But it is bigger than that. This movement, as Robert McRuer wrote about the LGBTQ movement, is both a rights movement and a radical liberation movement that "calls the system's bluff"—demanding not recognition but revolution. The fragility and fallibility of the human experience should be the basis of human rights.

I've learned that normality and ability are false judges of my worth, your worth, and our worth. We can be free of categories only when we live in specificity, see in specificity, love in specificity. I've learned that we will awaken from the dream and nightmare of the same only when we can value each other, care for each other, love each other, not as we should be, but as we are. And I've learned that, if loving people as they are, instead of how they should be, is what it means to awake from the dream of the same, then I am, even now, like so many of us, still dreaming.

———

My dad has never called me on the phone in my life. When I went away to college, he sent me "letters" that consisted of various newspaper clippings on topics he assumed I would be interested in. Stuff about the Dodgers and the Angels and my old soccer teams, political op-eds, updates on labor politics, mentions of Brown University in the news. Sometimes he would circle, underline, or highlight words, phrases, or sentences, or, if he was really emotive, draw arrows, happy faces, sad faces, and explosions. He never used words, with one exception: the letter he sent me every year on my birthday.

On March 19, without fail, I would receive a letter with various underlined and highlighted clippings but also a note that always said the same thing: "Still the best day of my life." On my forty-first birthday, after I hadn't heard from my dad in five years, he sent me a text with this string of emojis: ⚽ 😍 🎇 🎂

And then, *Still the best day of my life.*
I didn't respond.

Six months later, he texted me ✢⚡♥ and *want to have lunch sometime?*

My dad and I met at your uncle Bill's house—no one was home. I thought it would be a nice place to have lunch and talk. About what, I wasn't sure. It had been five years, and so much had been unsaid for so long, there could be no conversational middle ground. It would be either *Hey, how are you?* and *Nice day, huh?* or *Why the hell are you the way you are?* It could go either way.

My dad arrived in a black Honda Accord riddled with paint scratches and with a pockmarked bumper. My dad always crashes his cars. He pulled up to the front of the house but did not roll down his window to ask where to park. Instead, he proceeded to pantomime parking-related questions through the car window. Of course, asking me where to park with actual words would have been more efficient, but my dad has always gone to great lengths not to talk to other human beings. *Yes,* I signed back, *park there,* pointing to a spot across the narrow street from the house. *There?* he asked without asking but by pointing across the street. *Yes,* I said without saying it. *There?* he mouthed. *Yes,* I nodded. This went on for a few more minutes until he finally got it and drove to the end of the cul-de-sac, made a twenty-point turn, pulled back around, took a completely unnecessary parallel parking position (as there was no car in front of him), backed up, hit the car behind him, pulled forward, backed up, forward again, back again, forward once more, and then parked in the same place he'd started.

I don't have a lot of full memories of my dad, which I've read is common for children of alcoholics. The ones I do have are like frames from a movie left on the cutting room floor, out of sequence, without context, without story. I have only one picture of him, as my family took very few photos of any of us and no home movies, and this picture is my best memory of what he looked like. In this picture, I'm no more than two years old and I am sitting on his lap. I think we might be at Disneyland. I have on a white tank top with red stripes, my hair is Halloween orange and straw straight, cut to the exacting standards of a mixing bowl. My dad has thick, jet-black hair, a square jaw, an Irish potato nose, and caterpillar eyebrows. He is wearing a cool western shirt. He is holding me.

My dad got out of the car and his first words to me were, "It's 11:59. I'm early." My father liked to be early and used to say to me that if you aren't early, you're late, which I hated, because if you are early, you are early; on time, on time; and late, late. His hair was gray, he was at least three inches shorter than he'd been the last time I'd seen him, and he was hunched over from mid-spine like he had swallowed a bowling ball. He had on stonewashed Lee jeans, black Herman Munster shoes, and a brown shirt with food stains on the front. These stains were familiar, and I was immediately flooded with mental images of him driving me to soccer practice while drinking from a can of Progresso lentil soup, the brown water dripping down his chin and onto his shirt.

At the sight of my dad, my throat restricts and my chest tightens. I flex and release my neck muscles like a fish struggling to breathe on land. The back of my eyes itch and I turn them up toward the sky, attempting to roll them back into my head, as I did as a teenager, and hold them there as long as I can.

Turns out that my dad has brought his dog, Roscoe, with him. This is not a surprise, as much of my dad's emotional life has revolved around dogs. In fact, the final time my father went through detox, it was Roscoe that saved him. This was thirteen years ago, and I was living in New York and he was in California. For reasons unknown, my father decided to drink himself to death. He bought ten cases of Two-Buck Chuck from Trader Joe's, locked himself in his room, and did not eat or leave for a week. One night, my mom, who was (surprisingly) still married to my dad, found him on the floor of their apartment and called the paramedics.

He was revived in the ambulance, then admitted to the emergency room. My dad was not well cared for there. Somehow, he left the hospital still in his gown, in full detox, hallucinating. He believed that he had won the lottery and that a group of dognappers had dognapped Roscoe and were holding him for ransom. He was found later that day, searching for Roscoe and the winning lottery ticket on Wilshire Boulevard in Santa Monica. After a proper hospital stay, my dad enrolled in a recovery program. The fear of losing Roscoe, he told me later, helped him get sober. Credit where credit is due. And now, after a lifetime of alcohol abuse, my dad has been sober for more than a decade. Roscoe, I'm sure, has been his only friend through much of that time.

"I need to walk Roscoe" was the second thing my dad said to me that day, after not talking for five years. This request also did not come as a surprise. Taking the dog for a walk was a far more appropriate activity for us than having lunch. Every time my dad was fired, or the IRS came calling, or the money ran out, someone walked the dog. "Thanks for coming up here," I said as we walked. "Sure," he said. That was it. "So," I said after a few minutes of awkward silence, "what are you working on nowadays?" I knew this was the question to ask him, because my father, like many, I guess, changed when he talked about his work. My dad has always been deeply passionate about the work he did as an attorney. He went to law school to make money because that is what his mom told him he should do. He got a corporate law job in San Francisco that he eventually quit to, in his words, use his law degree to try to make the world a better place. As we walked, my dad told me all about a project he was working on to help immigrant families in Los Angeles. As he talked about ICE, the legality of sanctuary cities, immigration policy, he came alive. He became a different person from the one who had gotten out of the car.

We walked. He talked. I listened. Finally, I had to ask him, "Where have you been? Why did you disappear?" He didn't answer. I didn't ask this question in anger, but in sadness for what was and what could have been. I knew that there was so much good in him, not despite his differences but because of them. I knew the round parts of him had been squared, and the jagged parts shamed, and that he was wounded.

We stopped walking. My dad looked at me, then bent down toward Roscoe, who was panting and struggling to breathe. My dad stroked Roscoe's back, hugged his neck, and whispered something to him that I couldn't hear, and then I saw that he was crying. "Dunno," he finally said. "I guess if you look up the phase 'irreconcilable differences' in the dictionary you'll find a picture of me. I'm sorry."

When I was a kid, I thought my dad was ashamed of me. I was wrong. He was ashamed of himself. I could have ended up like my dad. I am like him in so many ways, but I did not become him, not despite of him, as I used to think, but because of him. When it mattered most, my father wasn't the dad I wanted, but he was the dad I needed. He practically quit his law practice to be my soccer coach when school got hard. Every Saturday he and I went to baseball games we couldn't afford, sitting five rows up from third base, getting there early to catch fly balls (though we never actually caught any), eating Subway sandwiches and Cracker Jack. He bought me as many baseball cards as I wanted—which we couldn't afford either—because I liked them, and we sat for hours talking about slugging percentages. And in sixth grade, when I was falling apart and had left school, under the lights in the parking lot of Dodger Stadium, sitting in our Aerostar van that smelled like wet dog and lentil soup, as I braced myself to be yelled at, told to buck up and work harder and go back to school, asked what was wrong with me for the thousandth time, my dad turned to me, and instead said, "I love you."

We walked back to his car and I asked him if he wanted

to come inside and have lunch. "Naaah," he said. "Have to get Roscoe home." He didn't say goodbye, or give me a hug. He just got back into his car, backed up, pulled forward, backed up, turned the wheel left, then right, then left, then rolled down his window. He leaned out. *Finally*, I thought. I walked over to the car, arms out for a hug, and he said, "Could you get Roscoe some water for the ride?" I did, and then he drove away.

What a mess. I wish it hadn't been, but it was. We humans are messy. I felt myself choke up and started to roll my eyes back again, like I'd done as a kid to escape. But I stood alone in the driveway and cried instead.

Later my dad texted me this: ♥♥🙏🐾🏄

I texted back: ♥

One morning when I was feeling anxious, I heard you singing to yourself in your bedroom. I sat outside your door and listened as you sang, "You got to feel it, you got to love it, you got to feel it, you got to love it." I opened your door and asked what you were singing about, and you said, "Life."

It was early, so I crept into your bed with a book. As I read to you, you interrupted me with rude comments about my receding hairline and graying beard, but you never laughed when I made so many mistakes as I read aloud. Even after all these years, I have to resist the urge to escape from reading out loud. When it is my turn to read at Seders, I excuse myself or pass the book to your mother. Or I ask you to read for "practice." I have been so ashamed, as an adult, as a father, that I've chased the horizon of normalcy. But with you, with us, I know that I am loved as I am.

This what we owe each other.

I want you to know what I am most proud of in my life. I'm proud that I was asked to contribute an essay for a book written by fifty alumni writers from Brown to celebrate the university's 250th anniversary. Four of those essays were chosen for a stage reading by actors at Lincoln Center. Mine was one of the four. It was called "The Dyslexic Brain Kicks Ass," because, even though it took me a long time to realize, Dave Cole was right.

I'm proud of your mom, whose interests and talents still radiate from her and won't be, can't be, squared. She is still the most complicated and complete sports-loving, screenplay-writing, public radio–producing, child-loving tough cookie I've ever known and is still my life, my love, after all these years.

I'm proud of my mom, who at seventy-five years old still runs her nonprofit organization and, of course, still curses like a truck driver.

I'm proud of my dad, who spent his life fighting for the vulnerable and who managed to reclaim himself from the abyss and create for himself a messy, imperfect life, which is the only way to live.

I'm proud that I proved so many people wrong. But I'm more proud that I proved my mom, my sisters, my brother, Mr. R, Father Young, Mr. T, Susan, Graciella, Robert, Dave, your mother, and my dad, who all believed in me, *right*.

I'm still dyslexic. I still can't sit still or find my car keys. I still can't spell. I still can't read out loud. I still struggle with the challenges and gifts of anxiety and depression. I haven't fixed myself. But I'm also not that kid who was so scared, so filled with shame, that I couldn't live a full life. Your mom and I have cared for each other for twenty years. I've been self-employed for twenty years, doing work I care about. I am a writer. I haven't destroyed myself like I thought I would, like I felt I had to. I'm proud of the life we live together and the person I've become.

Am I normal? No, I'm not. No one is. For so long I wanted so much to say yes, because I had wanted more than anything to be normal. But I don't anymore. Normal is like the horizon. The closer you get to it, the further away you are.

Normal has to be rejected and replaced with a relentless commitment to stop chasing this horizon and to escape the grasp of categories. It must be replaced with a way of living, an ethics of difference, that embraces the sharp edges, broken parts, and chipped facades of real people. This is the first step, the only step, toward loving people not for how they should be but for who they are.

Somewhere in human history, instead of being stable, our species experienced constant biological change and instead of being all the same, we are different. To be different is not the exception but the rule. It is our eccentricities, fallibility, vulnerability, our deviations from the norm—our differences—that constitute our humanity.

You have a choice to make about how to live your life. As

Henri-Jacques Stiker asked, will you choose a love of difference or chase the dream of the same? A love of differences is life. A desire for sameness is a denial of life. No human is normal, and the surest path to an unethical life is to forget that and force a way of being on anyone.

Those parts of yourself that might be called "not normal" have value, and those that fit the norm—your gender, class status, ability, skin color, and privilege—make you no better than anyone else. You must fight for the right of every person to be different, and even more forcefully when the differences being fought for are different from your own.

Normal is a false standard for human value to which I will not hold you, which can't hold you. I love you—all of you, the parts that bend, break, deviate, cause pain, bring joy—the concentric circles of self that radiate from you and can't be squared. My beautiful, essential and singular permutations of the species: You have a right to be free of normal. You have a right to be different.

Notes

I. Not Normal

3 Sons, You have each asked me a question: I was inspired to address this book to my sons by Ta-Nehisi Coates, *Between the World and Me* (New York: Spiegel & Grau, 2015); Omar Saif Ghobash, *Letters to a Young Muslim* (New York: Picador, 2016); and many other "activist" books written in letter form.

5 "The judges of normality": Michel Foucault, *Discipline and Punish: The Birth of the Prison* (New York: Pantheon, 1977), 304.

5 French anthropologist Claude Lévi-Strauss: Claude Lévi-Strauss, *Anthropologie structurale* (Paris: Plon, 1958; reprint, 1974), vol. 1, chap. 11, cited in Henri-Jacques Stiker, *A History of Disability*, trans. William Sayers (Ann Arbor: The University of Michigan Press, 1999), 48.

15 then came school, where I quickly became "one of *those kids*": This section was adapted from a previously published essay: Jonathan Mooney, "You Are Special! Now Stop Being Different," *New York Times*, October 12, 2017.

II. Normal Hasn't Always Been Normal

23 "whispers in your ear that what is normal is also all right": Ian Hacking, *The Taming of Chance* (Cambridge, UK: Cambridge University Press, 1990), 160.

24 Hacking was the first to point out: Hacking, *The Taming of Chance*, 162–64.

24 **an entire field of people who study this kind of stuff**: In addition to the three books mentioned, I most often refer to: Hacking, *The Taming of Chance*; Foucault, *Discipline and Punish* (New York: Pantheon, 1977); and Lennard J. Davis, *Enforcing Normalcy* (New York: Verso, 1995).

25 *normal* **is describing a fact in the world**: Hacking, *The Taming of Chance*, 162–64.

26 **So who used** *normal,* **and why, and how?**: My history of the uses of *normal* draws directly from Peter Cryle and Elizabeth Stephens, *Normality: A Critical Genealogy* (Chicago: The University of Chicago Press, 2017).

27 **they studied and defined its opposite—the pathological state**: Georges Canguilhem, *The Normal and the Pathological* (Brooklyn, NY: Zone Books, 1991); and Cryle and Stephens, *Normality*, chapter 1.

28 **a Swiss mathematician named Jakob Bernoulli**: Cryle and Stephens, *Normality*, 67–70.

28–31 **Fast forward a hundred years . . . according to Quetelet, the average man is the impossible man**: Cryle and Stephens, *Normality*, 69, 101, 109, 111, 114–141; and Davis, *Enforcing Normalcy*, 26–30.

29 **"If the average man were perfectly established"**: Adolphe Quetelet, *Sur l'homme et le développement de ses facultés on Essai de physique sociale*, 2 vols. (Paris: Bachelier, 1835), 2:266–67.

31 **Galton made significant changes in statistical theory**: Davis, *Enforcing Normalcy*, 33–34.

32 **"a practice of social and biological normalization"**: Cryle and Stephens, *Normality*, 232.

33 **So who were these people seeking out the normal in human form?**: Cryle and Stephens, *Normality*, 262–91.

36 **the Grant Study of Normal Young Men at Harvard**: Clark H. Heath, *What People Are; A Study of Normal Young Men*, The Grant Study, Department of Hygiene, Harvard University (Cambridge, MA: Harvard University Press, 1945); Cryle and Stephens, *Normality*, 309–12.

37 **By midcentury this new normal was set in stone:** Cryle and Stephens, *Normality*, 313–23.

38 **held a competition to find the living embodiment of Norma:** Julian B. Carter, *The Heart of Whiteness* (Durham, NC: Duke University Press, 2007).

39 **As Peter Cryle and Elizabeth Stephens rightly note:** Cryle and Stephens, *Normality*, 321.

III. Abnormal

48 **A philosopher I admire named Ron Mallon believes:** Ron Mallon, *The Construction of Human Kinds* (Oxford, UK: Oxford University Press, 2016).

49 **a looping effect where the person and the "problem" merge:** Ian Hacking, *The Social Construction of What?* (Cambridge, MA: Harvard University Press, 1999).

49 **people with cognitive and physical differences during the Middle Ages "were spontaneously part of a world":** Henri-Jacques Stiker, *A History of Disability*, trans. William Sayers (Ann Arbor: The University of Michigan Press, 1999), 65.

49 **Difference became abnormality:** Sharon L. Snyder and David T. Mitchell, *Cultural Locations of Disability* (Chicago: The University of Chicago Press, 2006).

51 **this was not an "objective" science of human variability:** Snyder and Mitchell, *Cultural Locations of Disability*, 193.

51 **physical anthropologists who pioneered anthropometric measurement:** Cryle and Stephens, *Normality*, 141–79.

51 **Take the work of Paul Broca:** Cryle and Stephens, *Normality*, 154.

52 **a field emerged in Italy known as criminal anthropology:** Cryle and Stephens, *Normality*, 180–84.

52 **along came psychometrics:** Cryle and Stephens, *Normality*, 212–55; Stephen J. Gould, *The Mismeasure of Man* (New York: W. W. Norton, 1996); Snyder and Mitchell, *Cultural Locations of Disability*; and James W. Trent, Jr., *Inventing the Feeble Mind* (Berkeley: University of California Press, 1995).

54 **In the mid-to-late 1800s, modern psychiatry was born:** Michel Foucault, *Abnormal: Lectures at the Collège de France, 1974–1975* (New York: Picador, 2003).

54 **At this time there is an expansion of categories, called "syndromes":** Foucault, *Abnormal*, 311.

54 **"physically, intellectually, and morally *abnormal* children":** Cryle and Stephens, *Normality*, 252.

54 **"runaway slave madness":** Samuel A. Cartwright, MD, "Report on the Diseases and Physical Peculiarities of the Negro Race," *New Orleans Medical and Surgical Journal*, May 1851, p. 707.

57 **Michel Foucault called the cultural systems and institutions that pathologize . . . the "normalizing society":** Michel Foucault, *Discipline and Punish: The Birth of the Prison* (New York: Pantheon, 1977); and Michel Foucault, *The History of Sexuality, Volume 1: An Introduction* (New York: Vintage Books, 1978), 144.

58 **"concerned with our growing capacities to control":** Nikolas Rose, *The Politics of Life Itself* (Princeton: Princeton University Press, 2007), 3.

58 **Ann Waldschmidt, a sociologist and disability theorist:** Ann Waldschmidt, "Who Is Normal? Who Is Deviant?" *Foucault and the Government of Disability*, ed. Shelley Tremain (Ann Arbor: The University of Michigan Press, 2005), 194.

58 **This type of society is organized to make us more alike than different:** David T. Mitchell with Sharon L. Snyder, *The Biopolitics of Disability* (Ann Arbor: The University of Michigan Press, 2015), 14.

58 **uses the statistical abstraction of normal as its organizing**

principle: Susan Wendell, *The Rejected Body* (New York: Routledge, 1996), 88–91; and Tobin Siebers, *Disability Theory* (Ann Arbor: The University of Michigan Press, 2008), 85.

59 The historian Henri-Jacques Stiker has described: Stiker, *A History of Disability*, 121–90.

60 students with physical impairments could be excluded from school: See Beattie v. Board of Ed. of Antigo, 169 Wis 231, 232, 172 N.W. 153 (1919).

60 "More than 1 million students were excluded from public school": "Back to School on Civil Rights: Advancing the Federal Commitment to Leave No Child Behind," National Council on Disability (January 25, 2000), 6.

60 Special education was, and still is, a bold idea that challenged deeply held beliefs: James W. Trent, Jr., *Inventing the Feeble Mind* (Berkeley: University of California Press, 1995), 144–54.

60 "should be a sieve through which those who will not be self-supporting": Florence G. Smith Fishbein, "Remarks on the Findings of the Mental Examinations of This Series of Eleven Children," *Eugenics and Social Welfare Bulletin* 15 (1913): 99.

65 differences of all kinds are turned into deficiencies: Snyder and Mitchell, *Cultural Locations of Disability*.

66 a boy named Michael liked to play with "girl" toys: Phyllis Burke, *Gender Shock: Exploding the Myths of Male and Female* (New York: Doubleday, 1996). Paraphrased from Kathryn Pauly Morgan's essay "Gender Police" in *Foucault and the Government of Disability*, ed. Shelley Tremain, 303.

66 a father's hearing treatment for his deaf daughter: Robert Carver, quoted in Fiona Kumari Campbell, "Legislating Disability," *Foucault and the Government of Disability*, ed. Shelley Tremain, 119.

71 A report by the National Disability Rights Network: *School Is Not*

Supposed to Hurt: Investigative Report on Abusive Restraint and Seclusion in Schools (Washington, DC: National Disability Rights Network, 2009), 14, 16, 21, 22, and 24. See also *Seclusions and Restraints: Selected Cases of Death and Abuse at Public and Private Schools and Treatment Centers*, GAO-09-719T (Washington, DC: U.S. Government Accountability Office, 2009).

72 **A report by the Ruderman Family Foundation:** I got most of these statistics from the Ruderman Family Foundation's white papers, which can be found here: See http://rudermanfoundation.org/advocacy-media /white-papers/; and Doris Zames Fleischer and Frieda Zames, *The Disability Rights Movement* (Philadelphia: Temple University Press, 2011).

73 **the lives of those with brain and body differences have been blighted:** Bill Hughes, "What Can a Foucauldian Analysis Contribute to Disability Theory?" *Foucault and the Government of Disability*, ed. Shelley Tremain, 83.

IV. Normed

79 **the purpose of the eugenics movement was simple:** Edwin Black, *War Against the Weak* (Washington, DC: Dialog Press, 2012); Edith Sheffer, *Asperger's Children* (New York: W. W. Norton & Company, 2018); Adam Cohen, *Imbeciles* (New York: Penguin Press, 2016); James W. Trent, Jr., *Inventing the Feeble Mind* (Berkeley: University of California Press, 1995); Sharon L. Snyder and David T. Mitchell, *Cultural Locations of Disability* (Chicago: The University of Chicago Press, 2006); Daniel J. Kevles, *In the Name of Eugenics* (New York: Alfred A. Knopf, 1985); and American Experience, "The Eugenics Crusade: What's Wrong with Perfect?" PBS, aired October 16, 2018, https://www .pbs.org/wgbh/americanexperience/films/eugenics-crusade/.

80 **Spencer believed that "all imperfection must disappear":** Herbert Spencer, *Social Statics* (New York: Robert Schalkenback Foundation, 1970 [1851]), 62.

81 **"Whenever you can, count":** Karl Pearson, *The Life, Letters and*

Labours of Francis Galton (Cambridge, UK: Cambridge University Press, 2011 [1930]), 232; and Francis Galton, *Memories of My Life* (New York: Routledge, 2015 [1908]), 315.

81 **"Could not the undesirables be got rid of and the desirables multiplied?":** Pearson, *The Life, Letters and Labours of Francis Galton,* 348.

82 **He called this eugenics:** Francis Galton, *Essays in Eugenics* (London: Eugenics Education Society, 1909); and Pearson, *The Life, Letters and Labours of Francis Galton.*

83 **Davenport was from the best genetic stock:** Black, *War Against the Weak,* 34.

84 **His mantra was "We need more protoplasm":** Black, *War Against the Weak,* 36.

84 **Davenport's big break came in 1902:** For more on the history of the Eugenics Records Office and Davenport see: Black, *War Against the Weak,* 36–41.

85 **"the registration of the genetic backgrounds of all Americans":** Black, *War Against the Weak,* 45.

85 **"the great strains for human protoplasm that are surging through the country":** Charles Benedict Davenport, *Heredity in Relation to Eugenics* (New York: Henry Holt and Company, 1911), 271; and C. B. Davenport, "Report of Committee on Eugenics," *Journal of Heredity* 6, no. 1 (January 1911): 91, 92.

85 **the "submerged 10th" of the normal curve:** Black, *War Against the Weak,* 52.

85 **Who were these defectives?:** Snyder and Mitchell, *Cultural Locations of Disability,* 78.

86 **Who else?:** Black, *War Against the Weak,* 58.

86 **To find the "defectives in our midst":** Black, *War Against the Weak,* 45.

Notes

86 **Fitter Families Contests:** Cohen, *Imbeciles*, 61.

87 **"The Best Practical Means for Cutting Off the Defective Germ-Plasms of the American Population":** Harry H. Laughlin, *Bulletin No. 10B: Report of the Committee to Study and to Report on the Best Practical Means of Cutting Off the Defective Germ-Plasm in the American Population* (Cold Spring Harbor, NY: Eugenics Records Office, 1914), 145.

87 **banned non-eugenic marriages:** Cohen, *Imbeciles*, 63.

87 **Next on the list: lock 'em up:** Trent, *Inventing the Feeble Mind*, 139, 140.

87 **"It is possible to colonize":** Snyder and Mitchell, *Cultural Locations of Disability*, 90.

88 **in 1967, the large public institutions . . . held nearly 200,300 defectives:** Trent, *Inventing the Feeble Mind*, 266.

88 **Utopia, however, these institutions were not:** Ella Morton, "Belchertown State School, a Horrific Home for the 'Feeble-Minded,'" *Slate*, July 7, 2015, http://www.slate.com/blogs/atlas_obscura/2014/07/07/abandoned_belchertown_state_school_for_the_feeble_minded_in_massachusetts.html; Trent, *Inventing the Feeble Mind*, 245; and Benjamin Ricci, *Crimes Against Humanity* (Lincoln, NE: iUniverse, Inc., 2004).

89 **"The ultimate aim of the school":** Trent, *Inventing the Feeble Mind*, 25, 219.

89 **within two months of admittance, 10 percent of those institutionalized died:** Black, *War Against the Weak*, 257.

90 **"calculations on the working out of a proposed program of sterilization":** Harry H. Laughlin, "Calculations on the Working Out of a Proposed Program of Sterilization" *Proceedings of the First National Conference on Race Betterment* (Battle Creek, MI: Race Betterment Foundation, 1914), 478.

90 **wasn't the first time sterilization had been proposed:** Cohen, *Imbeciles*, 7, 86.

90 **Dr. Hoyt Pilcher was the first in modern times to use castration as a way to prevent procreation:** Black, *War Against the Weak*, 63.

91 **Leaders of the optometry profession made a plan:** Black, *War Against the Weak*, 148.

91 **A school-to-operating-table pipeline was developed:** Sharon L. Snyder and David T. Mitchell, *Cultural Locations of Disability* (Chicago: The University of Chicago Press, 2006), 95.

91 **15 million people . . . as candidates for sterilization:** Cohen, *Imbeciles*, 118, 301.

92 **memorialized in a popular eugenics poem:** E. Carleton MacDowell, "Charles Benedict Davenport, 1866–1944: A Study of Conflicting Influences," *Bios* 17, no. 1 (March 1946): 30; and Cohen, *Imbeciles*, 77.

92 **A man named Buck Smith:** Bill McKelway, "Patient 'Assembly Line' Recalled by Sterilized Man," *Richmond Times-Dispatch*, February 24, 1980.

92 **the sterilization of a woman named Carrie Buck:** Cohen, *Imbeciles*, 97.

93 **The legality of Carrie Buck's sterilization:** *Buck v. Bell*, 274 U.S. 200 (1927), p. 67; quoted from: Black, *War Against the Weak*, 115.

94 **Almost seventy thousand people were sterilized:** Black, *War Against the Weak*, 254, 398.

94 **Vivian went on to become an honors student:** Cohen, *Imbeciles*, 7.

95 **"It would be an act of kindness and a protection":** Charles Henderson, "The Relation of Philanthropy to Social Order and Progress" *National Conference of Charities and Corrections: Proceedings of the Twenty-Sixth Annual Session* (Cincinnati, May, 1899), 4, cited by Curtis, 53, 55. "Propagation of the Unfit," *Institution Quarterly*, vol. 1 (May 1910), 35.

95 **Point eight of *The Best Practical Means*:** See Harry H. Laughlin, *Bulletin No. 10A: Report of the Committee to Study and to Report on the Best*

Practical Means of Cutting Off the Defective Germ-Plasm in the American Population (Cold Spring Harbor, NY: Eugenics Records Office, 1914), 45–46, 55, quoted in Black, *War Against the Weak*, 60, 247.

95 **in 1917, the movement got its own movie called** *The Black Stork*: Black, *War Against the Weak*, 257.

96 **Adolf Hitler . . . called a popular eugenics book "his bible":** Black, *War Against the Weak*, 259–260.

96 **a 1934 letter from C. M. Goethe:** Black, *War Against the Weak*, 258, 277.

96 **As the historian Edith Sheffer wrote, the Third Reich was a diagnosis regime:** Edith Sheffer, *Asperger's Children* (New York: W. W. Norton & Company, 2018), 18.

96 **On July 14, 1933, Germany issued a mass compulsory sterilization statute:** Cohen, *Imbeciles*, 10; and Black, *War Against the Weak*, 277, 299.

97 *Ausschusskinderer*, **or "garbage children":** Suzanne E. Evans, Forgotten Crimes: The Holocaust and People with Disabilities (Chicago: Ivan R. Dee, Publisher, 2004), 15–16; Sheffer, *Asperger's Children*, 20; Robert Jay Lifton, *The Nazi Doctors: Medical Killing and the Psychology of Genocide* (New York: Basic Books, 2017), 51; Henry Friedlander, *The Origins of Nazi Genocide: From Euthanasia to the Final Solution* (Chapel Hill: The University of Chapel Hill Press, 1995).

98 **"blood and spinal fluids were drawn while they were still alive":** Evans, *Forgotten Crimes*, 38.

98 **In October 1939, Hitler signed the order for the T4 Program:** Evans, *Forgotten Crimes*, 41–94; Friedlander, *The Origins of Nazi Genocide*.

98 **The killing program . . . was officially "halted" on August 24, 1941:** Evans, *Forgotten Crimes*, 17, 68–71.

99 **more than 750,000 "abnormal" or "defective" individuals were murdered:** Evans, *Forgotten Crimes*, 93.

99 **After the war . . . disabled victims were not recognized**: Evans, *Forgotten Crimes*, 158, 160; and Snyder and Mitchell, *Cultural Locations of Disability*, 125.

99 **"at least thirty eponymous neurological and psychiatric diagnoses"**: Sheffer, *Asperger's Children*, 18.

99 **Singer has referred to a disabled child as "it"**: Aaron Klein, "Interview with Peter Singer," 2015 (https://soundcloud.com/atfyfe/interview -with-peter-singer); and Peter Singer, *Practical Ethics* (Cambridge, UK: Cambridge University Press, 1979).

100 **Murphy wrote an article**: J. G. Murphy, "Do the Retarded Have a Right to be Eaten?" *Ethics and Mental Retardation*, ed. Loretta Kopelman and John C. Moskop, vol. 15 (1984): 43–46.

100 **More than 30 percent of individuals in prison**: Jennifer Bronson, Laura Maruschak, and Marcus Berzofsky, "Disabilities Among Prison and Jail Inmates, 2011–12," U.S. Department of Justice Special Report, December 2015, https://www.bjs.gov/content/pub/pdf/dpji1112.pdf.

100 **Most of the 376 eugenics departments . . . have become genetics departments**: Black, *War Against the Weak*, 411–26; Anne Kerr and Tom Shakespeare, *Genetic Politics: From Eugenics to Genome* (Cheltenham, UK: New Clarion Press, 2002); Snyder and Mitchell, *Cultural Locations of Disability*, 136; Rose, *The Politics of Life Itself*.

100 **Oregon ordered its last forced sterilization in 1981**: Cohen, *Imbeciles*, 11.

100 **Buck vs. Bell has never been overruled or limited**: Cohen, *Imbeciles*, 12.

100 **James Watson, the father of modern genetics**: Black, *War Against the Weak*, 442.

100 **Brain differences . . . described as possibly "curable"**: Harrison Wein, "Mental Disorders May Share Molecular Origins," NIH Research Matters, National Institutes of Health, February 27, 2018;

Aaron Rothstein, "Mental Disorder or Neurodiversity?" *The New Atlantis*, Number 36, Summer 2012, 99–115; Robert Gebelhoff, "What's the Difference Between Genetic Engineering and Eugenics?" *Washington Post*, February 22, 2016.

V. Act Normal

107 **"work the trap that one is inevitably in"**: Judith Butler, "The Body You Want," interview by Liz Kotz, *Artforum* (November 1992), https://www.artforum.com/print/previews/199209/the-body-you -want-an-inteview-with-judith-butler-33505.

112 **When you hide, not only do you live in fear, but also in shame**: My understanding of "disability passing" is inspired by Tobin Siebers's application of queer theory to disability in Tobin Siebers, *Disability Theory* (Ann Arbor: The University of Michigan Press, 2008), 96–119; Kenji Yoshino, *Covering: The Hidden Assault on Our Civil Rights* (New York: Random House, Inc., 2006); and Erving Goffman, *Stigma: Notes on the Management of Spoiled Identity* (New York: Simon & Schuster, 1993).

113 **"One is *something* in experiencing shame"**: Eve Kosofsky Sedgwick, *Touching Feeling: Affect, Pedagogy, Performativity* (Durham, NC: Duke University Press, 2003), 37.

129 **I dreamed of my self-worth in the symbols of power and privilege**: James Baldwin, *The Fire Next Time* (New York: Vintage Books, 1962), 79.

VI. Normal People Suck

138 **That night, all of the transfer students gathered**: This section was adapted from a previously published essay: Jonathan Mooney, "The Dyslexic Brain Kicks Ass," *The Brown Reader: 50 Writers Remember College Hill* (New York: Simon & Schuster, 2014).

147 **two seminal books by Alfred Kinsey**: Alfred Kinsey, *Sexual Behavior in the Human Male* (Bloomington, IN: Indiana University Press,

1975 [1948]); and Alfred Kinsey, *Sexual Behavior in the Human Female* (Bloomington, IN: Indiana University Press, 1997 [1953]).

150 **many other texts that rejected the medical model of disability**: In addition to the books mentioned in the text, I also recommend Simi Linton, *Claiming Disability* (New York: New York University Press, 1998).

154 **Normality, ability, disability are not features or facts inside a human being**: Books and articles on the social model for disability include Michael Oliver, *The Politics of Disablement* (New York: Palgrave Macmillan, 1990); Linton, *Claiming Disability*; Wendell, *The Rejected Body*; Rosemarie Garland Thomson, *Extraordinary Bodies: Figuring Physical Disability in American Culture and Literature* (New York: Columbia University Press, 1997); Tom Shakespeare, *Disability Rights and Wrongs* (New York: Routledge, 2006); and Kristjana Kristiansen, Simo Vehmas, and Tom Shakespeare, ed., *Arguing About Disability* (New York: Routledge, 2009).

159 **to protest, to resist, to heal is to reject the false claims made about you**: Tobin Siebers, *Disability Theory* (Ann Arbor: The University of Michigan Press, 2008), 19.

160 **It is what Foucault called a "transactional reality"**: Michel Foucault, *The Birth of Biopolitics: Lectures at the Collège de France, 1978–1979* (New York: Picador, 2004), 297.

VII. The New Normal

164 **as normal changes, its power over us stays the same**: Michael Warner, *The Trouble with Normal: Sex, Politics, and the Ethics of Queer Life* (Cambridge, MA: Harvard University Press, 2000); David T. Mitchell with Sharon L. Snyder, *The Biopolitics of Disability* (Ann Arbor: The University of Michigan Press, 2015); Jürgen Link, "Standard Deviation," interview with Anne Mihan and Thomas O. Haakenson, *Cabinet Magazine* 15 (Fall 2004), http://www.cabinetmagazine.org/issues/15/mihan_haakenson.php; and Robert McRuer, *Crip Theory* (New York: New York University Press, 2006).

170 **Each new edition of the *Diagnostic Statistical Manual*:** Lennard J. Davis, *The End of Normal* (Ann Arbor: The University of Michigan Press, 2013), 63; Peter Conrad, *The Medicalization of Society* (Baltimore: Johns Hopkins University Press, 2007); Susan Cain, *Quiet* (New York: Crown Publishers, 2012); Allan V. Horwitz and Jerome C. Wakefield, *The Loss of Sadness* (New York: Oxford University Press, 2007); Bradley Lewis, *Moving Beyond Prozac, DSM, and the New Psychiatry: The Birth of Postpsychiatry* (Ann Arbor: University of Michigan Press, 2006); Ray Moynihan and Alan Cassels, *Selling Sickness* (New York: Nation Books, 2005).

170 **New York University's Child Study Center . . . launched a national PSA campaign:** Joanne Kaufman, "Ransom-Note Ads About Children's Health Are Canceled," *New York Times*, Dec. 20, 2007, https://www.nytimes.com/2007/12/20/business/media/20child.html/.

173 **my ability to approximate a "specific expectation of normalcy":** David T. Mitchell with Sharon L. Snyder, *The Biopolitics of Disability* (Ann Arbor: The University of Michigan Press, 2015), 14, 59, 104.

180 **an industry-wide standard for clothing sizes:** Peter Cryle and Elizabeth Stephens, *Normality: A Critical Genealogy* (Chicago: The University of Chicago Press, 2017), 325.

181 **"variation is an inherent and integral part of the human—or indeed any—genome":** Matt Ridley, *Genome: The Autobiography of a Species in 23 Chapters* (New York: HarperPerennial, 2006), 145.

181 **"it's not so categorical as: this is normal, this is abnormal":** Gail Saltz, M.D., *The Power of Different* (New York: Flatiron Books, 2017), 211.

181 **the world's largest study of disability, ability, and typical functioning:** World Health Organization, *World Report on Disability* (Geneva, Switzerland: WHO Press, 2011), http://www.who.int/disabilities/world_report/2011/report.pdf.

182 **half of all people will experience a mental health challenge:** Tay-

lor Knopf, "CDC: 'Nearly 50% of U.S. Adults will Develop at Least One Mental Illness,'" CNSNews, June 13, 2013, https://www.cnsnews.com/ news/article/cdc-nearly-50-us-adults-will-develop-least-one-mental-ill- ness; "Mental Disorders Affect One in Four People," World Health Report, World Health Organization, 2001, https://www.who.int/ whr/2001/media_centre/press_release/en; "The State of LD: Under- standing the 1 in 5," National Center for Learning Disabilities, May 2, 2017, https://www.ncld.org/archives/blog/the-state-of-ld-understand- ing-the-1-in-5; Jon Baio, Lisa Wiggins, Deborah L. Christensen, et al., "Prevalence of Autism Spectrum Disorder Among Children Aged 8 Years—Autism and Developmental Disabilities Monitoring Network, 11 Sites, United States, 2014," *Surveillance Summaries*, April 27, 2018, 67(6), 1–23, http://dx.doi.org/10.15585/mmwr.ss6706a1.

VIII. Normal People Are People You Don't Know Very Well

185 **Normal People Are People You Don't Know Very Well:** The title of this chapter is a paraphrase of a quote usually attributed to Alfred Adler: "The only normal people are the ones you don't know very well." *Normal People Are People You Don't Know That Well* is also the title of a comedy album by Jackie Martling.

188 **Every society has struggled and failed to integrate:** Stiker, *A History of Disability*, 192.

189 **a beautiful essay called "Escape from Shame":** Tammy S. Thomp- son, "Escape from Shame," *Mouth Magazine* 43 (July 1997).

194 **a growing number of interdisciplinary researchers:** Thomas Armstrong, PhD, *Neurodiversity: Discovering the Extraordinary Gifts of Autism, ADHD, Dyslexia, and Other Brain Differences* (Cambridge, MA: Da Capo Press, 2010); Gail Saltz, MD, *The Power of Different: The Link Between Disorder and Genius* (New York: Flatiron Books, 2017); Steve Silberman, *NeuroTribes: The Legacy of Autism and the Future of Neurodiversity* (New York: Avery, 2015).

195 **Research has finally caught up with Jim:** for an overview of

research on autism and talent, see Teresa Iuculano et al., "Brain Organization Underlying Superior Mathematical Abilities in Children with Autism," *Biological Psychiatry* 75, no. 3 (February 2014): 223–30; Emma Ashwin et al., "Eagle-Eyed Visual Acuity: An Experimental Investigation of Enhanced Perception in Autism," *Biological Psychiatry* 65, no. 1 (January 2009): 17–21; Fabienne Samson et al., "Enhanced Visual Functioning in Autism: An ALE Meta-analysis," *Human Brain Mapping* 33, no. 7 (July 2012): 1553–81; Simon Baron-Cohen et al., "Talent in Autism: Hyper-Systemizing, Hyper-Attention to Detail and Sensory Hypersensitivity," *Philosophical Transactions of the Royal Society B* 364, no. 1522 (May 2009): 1377–83; Francesca Happe and Pedro Vital, "What Aspects of Autism Predispose to Talent?" *Philosophical Transactions of the Royal Society B* 364, no. 1522 (May 2009): 1369–75; Mary Ann Winter-Messiers, "From Tarantulas to Toilet Brushes: Understanding the Special Interests of Youth with Asperger Syndrome," *Remedial and Special Education* 28, no. 3 (May–June 2007): 140–52.

196 **A recent case study at SAP found**: Robert D. Austin and Gary P. Pisano, "Neurodiversity as a Competitive Advantage," *Harvard Business Review* 95, no. 3 (May–June 2017): 96–103.

197 **people with learning differences had larger right hemispheres**: S. E. Shaywitz, et al., "Functional Disruption in the Organization of the Brian for Reading in Dyslexia," *Proceedings of the National Academy of Sciences* 95 (1998): 2636–41; Sara G. Tarver, Patricia S. Ellsworth, and David J. Rounds, "Figural and Verbal Creativity in Learning Disabled and Nondisabled Children," *Learning Disability Quarterly* 3 (Summer, 1980): 11–18; Catya von Karolyi et al., "Dyslexia Linked to Talent: Global Visual-Spatial Ability," *Brain and Language* 85 (2003): 430; Gadi Geiger et al., "Wide and Diffuse Perceptual Modes Characterize Dyslexics in Vision and Audition," *Perception* 37, no. 11 (2008): 1745–64; Ulrika Wolff and Ingvar Lundberg, "The Prevalence of Dyslexia Among Art Students," *Dyslexia: An International Journal of Research and Practice* 8, no. 1 (Jan/Mar 2002): 34–42; Brent Bowers, "Study Shows Stronger Links Between Entrepreneurs and Dyslexia," *New York Times*, November 5, 2007; Julie Logan, "Dyslexic Entrepre-

neurs: The Incidence, Their Coping Strategies, and Their Business Skills," *Dyslexia: An International Journal of Research and Practice* 15 no. 4 (November 2009): 328–48.

198 **attention differences are clearly linked to creativity and originality:** See Harry Kimball, "Hyper-focus: The Flip Side of ADHD?" Child Mind Institute, Sept 23, 2013; Francisco X. Castellanos and Erika Proal, "Large-scale Brain Systems in ADHD: Beyond the Prefrontal-striatal Model," *Trends in Cognitive Science* 16 (January 2012); Anna Abraham et al., "Creative Thinking in Adolescents with Attention Deficit Hyperactivity Disorder (ADHD)," *Child Neuropsychology* 12, no. 2 (2006); Bonnie Cramond, "Attention-Deficit Hyperactivity Disorder and Creativity—What Is the Connection?" *The Journal of Creative Behavior* 28, no. 3 (August 2006): 44–54; "Daydreaming Boosts Creativity, Study Says," *Huffington Post*, October 20, 2012.

199 **impulsivity, hyperactivity, and creativity are all linked:** Dsrya Zabelina et al., "Do Dimensional Psychopathy Measures Relate to Creative Achievement or Divergent Thinking?" *Frontiers in Psychology* 5, no. 1029 (2014), doi:10.3389/fpsyg.2014.01029.

199 **the science of neurodiversity has advanced:** See Brendan Bradley et al., "Attention Bias for Emotional Faces in Generalized Anxiety Disorder," *British Journal of Clinical Psychology* 38, no. 3 (1999): 267–78; Jeremy D. Coplan et al., "The Relationship Between Intelligence and Anxiety: An Association with Subcortical White Matter Metabolism," *Frontiers in Evolutionary Neuroscience* 3, no. 8 (February 2012); Tiffany Szu-Ting Fu et al., "Confidence Judgment in Depression and Dysphoria: The Depressive Realism vs. Negativity Hypothesis," *Journal of Behavior Theory and Experimental Psychiatry* 43, no. 2 (June 2012): 699–704; Connie M. Strong et al., "Temperament-Creativity Relationships in Mood Disorder Patients, Healthy Controls and Highly Creative Individuals," *Journal of Affective Disorders* 100, nos. 1–3 (June 2007): 41–48; Jane Collingwood, "The Link Between Bipolar Disorder and Creativity," *Psych Central* (2016), accessed March 28, 2018.

200 **above-average IQ and creativity:** Eric C. Tully et al., "Quadratic

Associations Between Empathy and Depression as Moderated by Emotion Dysregulation," *Journal of Psychology* 150, no. 1 (2016): 15–35.

200 **decade-long study of writers**: Nancy C. Andreasen, "The Relationship Between Creativity and Mood Disorders," *Dialogues in Clinical Neuroscience* 10, no. 2 (June 2008): 251–55.

200 **"studies of the entire population of Iceland"**: John L. Karlsson, "Psychosis and Academic Performance," *British Journal of Psychiatry* 184 (2004): 327–329; Karlsson, "Genetic Association of Giftedness and Creativity with Schizophrenia," *Hereditas* 66, no. 2 (1970): 177–183, quoted from Thomas Armstrong, *Neurodiversity* (Cambridge, MA: Da Capo Press, 2010), 164.

201 **"Neurodiversity may be every bit as crucial for the human race"**: Harvey Blume, "Neurodiversity," *The Atlantic* (September 1998).

202 **I was rereading a book I had picked up at Brown called *The Rejected Body***: Susan Wendell, *The Rejected Body* (New York: Routledge, 1996), pp. 69 and 84.

204 **inhabit the world as an "innovative, embodied being"**: Mitchell and Snyder, *The Biopolitics of Disability*, 7.

206 **Difference and disability are not an exception to the rule**: Henri-Jacques Stiker, *A History of Disability*, trans. William Sayers (Ann Arbor: The University of Michigan Press, 1999); Martha C. Nussbaum, *Frontiers of Justice* (Cambridge, MA: Harvard University Press, 2006).

206 **Mutual care is a basic need of all humans**: Eva Feder Kittay and Ellen K. Feder, eds., *The Subject of Care: Feminist Perspectives on Dependency* (Lanham, MD: Rowman & Littlefield Publishers, 2002); Tobin Siebers, *Disability Theory* (Ann Arbor: The University of Michigan Press, 2008), 182.

207 **I've learned from Henri-Jacques Stiker**: Stiker, A *History of Disability*, 3.

216 **To be different is not the exception but the rule**: This paragraph

was inspired by David Horrobin, *The Madness of Adam and Eve: How Schizophrenia Shaped Humanity* (London: Bantam Press, 2001), 237.

217 **will you choose a love of difference or chase the dream of the same?:** Stiker, *A History of Disability*, 11.

217 **Normal is a false standard for human value:** Mitchell and Snyder, *The Biopolitics of Disability*, 134.

217 **permutations of the species:** Mitchell and Snyder, *The Biopolitics of Disability*, 136.

Acknowledgments

When you are dyslexic, like I am, and you spell at a third-grade level, like I do, and you write a book, like I have, there are oh so many people to thank. Those people who are thanked below, please know, that when you have felt for much of your life, like I did, deficient and defective, this thank you means everything. Most importantly, thank you to my wife, Rebecca, who is one tough cookie. Nothing is possible without her. To my children, the purpose for it all. I love you. To my mom, Colleen, the catalyst for it all; my father, the dad I needed when I was most in need; my sister Kelly, for always helping me imagine a different future from our past; my sister Michele, for her quiet courage; my brother, Billy, for his example. To Jill Kneerim for the past twenty years and Lucy V. Cleland for twenty more. To all the people who changed the way I think at Brown University. Thank you to all the writers, scholars, activists, and artists whose ideas are the heart and soul of this book, including Henri-Jacques Stiker, Sharon Snyder and David Mitchell, Shelley Tremain, Tammy S. Thompson, Tobin Siebers, Edith Sheffer, Suzanne Evans, Lennard J. Davis, Simi Linton, Peter Cryle and Elizabeth Stephens, Edwin Black, Susan Wendell, Rosemarie Garland

Thomson (The Great RGT), Pedro Noguera, Maryann Wolf, Tom Shakespeare, Gail Saltz, Thomas Armstrong, David Flink, The Eye-To-Eye Mafia, and to the millions of others who fight every day for a more inclusive world and everyone's right to be different. To the people who hosted me in their homes after I graduated from Brown and to all who shared their stories with me on the short bus. To my dedicated, critical, and insightful manuscript readers—Eli Wolf, Barb Buswell, David Connor, Sarah Everhart Skeels—your insights made this a better book and me a better writer, thinker, advocate. To Peter Catapano, *New York Times* opinion editor, for including me in his thoughtful and radical essay series on disability and Judy Sternlight for the great honor of contributing to the *Brown Reader*. To the amazing team at Henry Holt: Gillian Blake for taking the first meeting, Maggie Richardson for not making fun of how much older I look since the last time, Patricia Eisemann for seeing the big picture, Kathleen Cook, who is one hell of a copy editor, and of course, Libby Burton, who, despite the fact that she does not own a fax machine, was and is a writer's dream editor.

And lastly, thank you to whoever invented spell check.

About the Author

Chris Mueller

JONATHAN MOONEY's work has been featured in *The New York Times*, *The Los Angeles Times*, the *Chicago Tribune*, *USA Today*, HBO, NPR, ABC News, *New York* magazine, *The Washington Post*, and *The Boston Globe*. A nationally recognized advocate for neurological and physical diversity, he's been speaking across the nation about neurological and physical diversity for two decades, inspiring those who live with differences and calling for change. He has published two other books: *The Short Bus* and *Learning Outside the Lines*.